I0027639

Ancient Egypt & The Myth Of The White Pharaohs

Who Should I believe: You, Or My Lying Eyes..?

Truth B. Tole

Copyright © 2022 Truth B. Tole

All rights reserved.

ISBN: 978-0-578-39677-4

DEDICATION

This book is dedicated to all of the warrior scholars who have come before me. I have stood on their shoulders to get a glimpse of the past and the truth. The time and energy it must have taken the old school scholars to painstakingly gather their evidence one shred at a time still amazes me.

I am fortunate to live in the information age with knowledge and information at my fingertips. They did not have this luxury and presented this valuable information at a time when it was not fashionable to do so.

So, to the old school warrior scholars: Dr. Ben, Ivan Van Sertima, Frances Cress Welsing, Professor James Smalls, John G. Jackson, Leonard Jefferies, Drusilla Dunjee Houston, Carter G Woodson, J.A. Rogers, John Henrik Clarke, Cheikh Anta Diop, and George G.M. James, I say thank you.

To the new school historians and presenters of truth such as Dr. Umar Johnson, Robin Walker, Brother Akala, Charles Clark, Reggie Mabry, Kaba Kamene, Brother Saku, Brother Shaka, Anthony Browder, all of the presenters in the "Hidden Colors" documentaries and all of the scholars and reseachers bringing the truth to the forefront today, I also say thank you. We must keep passing the torch. This is not a sprint it is a marathon.

I must also take a moment to acknowledge other scholars such as Robert Bauval, Thomas Brophy and Jane Elliot who have been courageous enough to speak the truth as well.

I am forever indebted to all of you. You have opened my eyes and made this book possible. A thousand pardons to anyone I left out. Please check the "suggested readings" section at the back of this book for additional information.

The African Proverb says, "Until the lions have their own historians, tales of the hunt shall always glorify the hunter." I will make my best attempt to represent the lion throughout the pages of this book.

TABLE OF CONTENTS

ACKNOWLEDGEMENTS

I must acknowledge and give thanks to my family and friends for their continued support: Joy, Cherry, Tee, Brittany, Gigi, Elsie, Antoinette, Chanda, Levi, Grace, Dalana, Cheryl, Adonis, Rick and Anna. It is an honor for me to be a part of your lives and I give thanks to the universe that you are all a part of my life. To My mother, father and brother, I miss you.

Chapter I
The Lie

"If you tell a lie big enough and keep repeating it, people will
eventually come to believe it"

- Joseph Goebbels -

In various Hollywood movies, television shows and other forms of media, we see the ancient Egyptians portrayed as Europeans. We have all seen these images in old school movies such as "The Ten Commandments" or modern movies like "The Mummy" and "Gods Of Egypt". Even popular childrens books, cartoons, and movies show the ancient Egyptians as Europeans. These portrayals have stuck in our conscious and subconscious minds, but, the truth is, they are factually incorrect and should be addressed.

The damage that this misinformation does to young black boys and girls egos and self worth cannot be measured. Think of the difference it would make for these children to know that their ancestors, black people, laid the foundation for the sciences, agriculture, ship building, writing, astronomy, medicine, surgery, philosophy, metallurgy, architecture, religion, math, establishing laws and so much more. This reality, however, goes against the accepted racist narrative that black people have never contributed anything to society when, in fact, black people have laid the foundation and were the pioneers of so many of the disciplines that are studied today.

In this presentation, we will visit the issue of the ancient Egyptians from a common sense point of view and present images that support the fact that the ancient Egyptians were black and brown people from Africa. In the end, we ask a simple question. If you saw the people in this book walking down the street today, would you consider them black, a person of color or white?

Considering the tangible proof readily available that the ancient Egyptians left behind such as statues, carvings and paintings, it is amazing that this topic is still being debated. It is clear that the old racist and outdated representations and ideologies of the early Egyptologists persists to this day. This is unfortunate. Some of the claims that mainstream egyptologists, archaeologists and historians of the past, and present, have made to deny modern blacks/Africans of their rich ancient heritage will stretch your imagination. Others are outright laughable.

For instance, Champollion-Figeac, the brother of Champollion the Younger who deciphered the Hieroglyphic writing using the rosetta stone stated that, "The two physical traits of black skin and kinky hair are not enough to stamp a race as negro..."[1]

Allow that to sink in for a moment... "The two physical traits of black skin and kinky hair are not enough to stamp a race as negro..."

This statement was made in response to CF Volneys description of the ancient Egyptians as black people.[2]

Another example of a person in a position of authority going out of their way to discredit Africans/Black people is Zahi Hawass, the former minister of state for antiquities affairs of Egypt. He has said that, "although Egypt is in Africa, Egyptians are not black or African"[3]. Allow that to sink in also and think about that statement logically.

That is the equivalent of saying that although California and New York are in America, people who live in those states are not Americans; or that although Beijing is in China that the people who live in Beijing are not Chinese. Or, to take it a step further, it is like saying that although Cairo is in Egypt, the people who live in present day Cairo are not Egyptians. Obviously, Mr. Hawass does not want to be identified as African.

He went on to further say, "We believe that the origins of the ancient Egyptians were purely Egyptian based on a discovery made by British Egyptologist Flinders Petrie in Nakada, and that is why ancient Egyptian civilization did not take place in Africa, it only happened here,"[4] Where is here..? Although some people, because of racism and/or other motives, would like to take Egypt out of Africa, That is an impossible task.

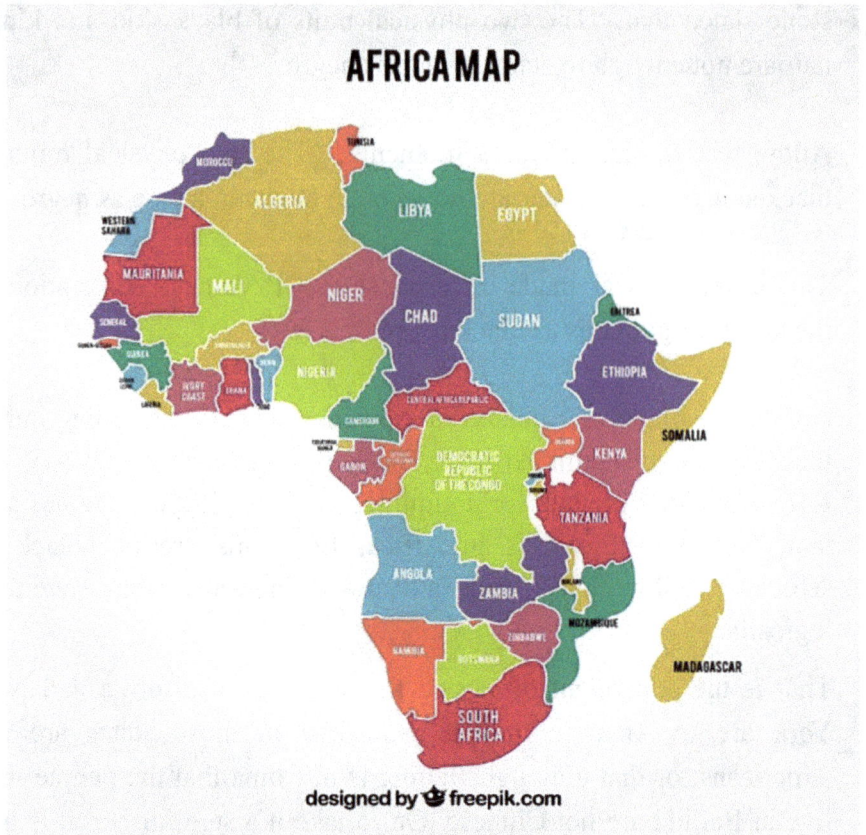

AFRICA MAP

designed by freepik.com

Image 1
Map Of Africa

Some people will claim that Egypt is not in Africa but in the "Middle East". When we unpack this, we understand that the term "Middle East" is a modern one that came into use in 1901. The ancient Egyptians, Greeks, Romans or any other culture of antiquity never referred to Egypt or the Egyptians as being from or in the "Middle East".

Mr. Hawass would have you suspend your reality even further and believe that the following images carved in stone are not black or African. Have a look, and please, apply your own common sense...

Image 2
-Pharaoh Narmer -
United Upper and Lower
Egypt. founded the First
Egyptian Dynasty.

Image 3
-Pharaoh Sahure -
Fifth Egyptian Dynasty.
Metropolitan Museum Of
Art, New York

Image 4
-Pharaoh Mentuhotep II-
Founded The Middle
Kingdom
Cairo Museum, Egypt.

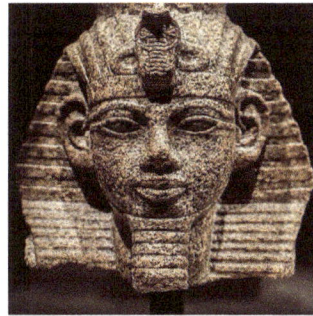

Image 5
-Pharaoh Amenhotep III-
18th Dynasty
Cairo Museum, Egypt.

Image 6
-Pharaoh Akhenaten-
18th Dynasty
Tutankhamun Exhibition,
Seattle WA

Image 7
-Pharaoh Tiharka-
The 25th Dynasty.
Ny Carlsberg Glyptotek,
Copenhagen

We can clearly see that from Egypt's earliest dynasties, the ancient Egyptians presented themselves as black or brown people with African features.

Chapter 2
The Ancient Historians

The view that the ancient Egyptians were not black or from Africa is a relatively modern one. The ancient historians and philosophers, absent the racism of today, described the ancient Egyptians as black and brown people.

Herodotus, who was an ancient Greek writer, geographer and historian is known for having written the "Histories" and is considered to be the Greek "Father Of History". He visited Egypt during the Persian occupation and stated that, "the Greeks were one of the first groups of foreigners that ever lived there".[5] Herodotus himself used the word "foreigner " when describing the Greeks in Egypt.

When describing the Greek oracle, Dodona, Herodotus goes on to say that, "The oracle was founded when two black doves flew from Thebes in Egypt". Herodotus further stated "she was known to be from Egypt because she was "black", Herodotus states that the natives of the Nile region are "black with heat", and that Egyptians were "black skinned with woolly hair".[6]

Another quote from Herodotus says, "...the Colchians are Egyptians by race....the Colchians were descended from soldiers of Sesostris (Senusret III, an Egyptian Pharoah). I had conjectured as much myself from two pointers, firstly because they have black skins and kinky hair.... and secondly and more reliably for the reason that alone among mankind the Egyptians and the Ethiopians have practiced circumcision since time immemorial... As between the Egyptians themselves and the Ethiopians I could not say which taught the other the practice for among them it is quite clearly a custom of great antiquity." [6]

Image 8
-Pharaoh Senusret III-
12th Dynasty
Munich Museum

Image 9
Soldiers from ancient Egypt
-11th Dynasty-
Egyptian Museum, Cairo

Aeschylus, the first of classical Athens great dramatists describing ancient Egyptians sailors stated, "I can see the crew with their black limbs and white tunics".[7]

Image 10
-Ancient Egyptian Sailors-
Taken From The Tomb Of Menna
Scribe Of The King
18th Dynasty

Image 11
-Ancient Egyptian Sailors-
Cairo Museum
Egypt, Africa

Lucian, The Greek satirical writer describing an Egyptian stated, "This boy is not merely black; he has thick lips and his legs are too thin...". [7]

Image 12
-Pharaoh Tutankhamun-
18th Dynasty
Museum Of Fine Arts,
Boston

Image 13
-Princess Of Pharaoh
Akhenaten's Family-
18th Dynasty
Louvre Museum
France

Apollodorus, another Greek philosopher said, "Aegyptos conquered the country of the black footed ones and called it Egypt after himself".[8] The ancient Egyptians called their land Kemet, meaning "The Black Land" or "Land Of The Blacks".

Diogenes of Sinope was an ancient Greek philospher and one of the founders of the Cynics. He said the following about Zeno the founder of the stoic school, "Appolonius of Tyre says of him that he was gaunt, very tall and black, hence the fact that, according to Chrysippus in the First Book of his proverbs, certain people called him an Egyptian vine-shoot".[9]

Constance deVolney who traveled to Egypt between 1783-1785, at the peak of the slave trade, made the following statement when describing the ancient Egyptians, "That this race of blacks who nowadays are slaves and the objects of our scorn is the very one to which we owe our arts, our sciences and even the use of spoken word".[10]

Ammianus Marcellinus was a Roman historian who wrote a history of the Roman world from 96 to 378. He wrote the following "The men of Egypt are mostly brown or black with a skinny and dessicated look."[11]

Aristotle is considered one of the greatest philosophers of all time and was a tutor to Alexander the Great. He stated that, "Those who are too black are cowards, like for instance, the Egyptians and Ethiopians. But those who are excessively white are also cowards... ".[12]

Diodorus of Siculus said, "They say also that the Egyptians are colonists sent out by the Ethiopians, Osiris having been the leader of the colony....."[13]

Image 14
-Ancient Egyptian Craftsmen At Work-
Metropolitan Museum Of Art
New York

When it comes to the ancient historians there was never any confusion as to the race of the people of ancient Egypt. They saw them and described them as they saw them, black and brown people.

Some facts to consider:

- **circa 7000 BCE** - Settlement of Nile Valley begins.

- **circa 3000 BCE** - Kingdoms of Upper and Lower Egypt are united under Pharaoh Narmer. Successive dynasties witness flourishing trade, prosperity and the development of great cultural traditions. Writing, including hieroglyphics, is used as an instrument of state. Construction of the pyramids - around 2,500 BC - is a formidable engineering achievement.

- **669 BCE** - Assyrians from Mesopotamia conquer and rule Egypt

- **525 BCE** - Persian conquest of Egypt

- **332 BCE** - Alexander the Great, of ancient Macedonia, conquers Egypt, founds Alexandria. A Macedonian dynasty rules until 31 BC.

- **31 BCE** - Egypt comes under Roman rule; Queen Cleopatra commits suicide after Octavian's army defeats her forces.

Note, when Alexander The Great invaded Egypt in 332 BC the pyramids in Egypt were already thousands of years old.

When it comes to Rome, it is often said that we are closer in time to the ancient Romans and Cleopatra than the ancient Romans were to the pyramid builders. This makes it mathematically impossible for the Greeks or Romans to have played any role in the founding of Egypt or any of its dynasties.

"We were trained to despise ourselves and all of Africa. We felt like Africans were either primitive or semi-primitive, that they had no science and made no significant contributions to civilization. We did not realize that we were looking at a looted Africa, a shattered Africa. We did not realize that there were two Africas, Africa before and after the Holocausts."

- Dr. Ivan Van Sertima -

CHAPTER 3
WHERE DID THE ANCIENT EGYPTIANS COME FROM

Some modern historians and egyptologist will say that no one knows where the ancient Egyptians came from. This seems to be misleading.

When it comes to the African origin of Egyptian civilization, one needs to look no further than what the ancient Egyptians said about themselves. They called their land Kamit, Kmt, Kemet, i.e., "the Black Land," or "Land Of The Blacks", and their own name for themselves was "Kamiu," which translates literally as "the Blacks."

The Egyptian's word for the African lands to the south of them was "Khenti" -- "Khentiu" denoting the Sudanic peoples who lived there -- and this is also their word for "first, foremost, beginning, origin and chief."[14]

Mainstream historians interpret Kemet to mean "the black land" referencing the soil - yes, "the soil" and not "land of the blacks" referencing the people who inhabited the land.

Be that as it may, we will clearly demonstrate that the ancient egyptians painted and represented themselves as black and brown African people with distinct African features. They did not paint or represent themselves as white or with European features or as any other race other than black/African people.

Diodorus of Siculus, referring to the Egyptian priests of Egypt says. "They say also that the Egyptians are colonists sent out by the Ethiopians, Osiris having been the leader of the colony... and the larger part of the customs of the Egyptians are, they hold, Ethiopian, the colonists still preserving their ancient manners. For instance, the belief that their kings are gods, the very special attention which they pay to their burials, and many other matters of a similar nature are Ethiopian practices, while the shapes of their statues and the forms of their letters are Ethiopian; for of the two kinds of writing which the Egyptians have, that which is known as 'popular' (demotic) is learned by everyone, while that which is called 'sacred' is understood only by the priests of the Egyptians, who learn it from their fathers as one of the things which are not divulged, but among the Ethiopians everyone uses these forms of letters......" [14]

In ancient times, the land south of Egypt (ancient Kush, modern day Sudan) was known to the ancient world by many names: Ta-Seti, (Land of the Bow, so named because the inhabitants were expert archers); Ta-Nehesi (Land of Copper); Ethiopia (Land of Burnt Faces, from the Greeks); Nubia (derived from an ancient Egyptian word for gold, which was plentiful) and Kush.

In some religious traditions, Kush was linked to the biblical Cush, son of Ham and grandson of Noah, whose descendants inhabited northeast Africa.[15]

The people of this region referred to themselves as Beja or Medjay. The same Medjay that became the police force in ancient Egypt. By the Eighteenth Dynasty the Medjay were an elite paramilitary police force.[16]

Over time, the word Medjay became synonymous with policing in general. As an elite police force, the Medjay were often used to protect valuable areas, especially areas of pharaonic interest like capital cities, royal cemeteries, and the borders of Egypt.

Although the Medjay were best known for their protection of the royal palaces and tombs in Thebes and the surrounding areas, the Medjay were used throughout Upper and Lower Egypt as well. Each regional unit had its own captains.[17]

Pharaohs

The ancient Egyptians did not refer to their Kings as Pharaohs. They referred to their leader as King. They considered their King to be the most important and powerful person in the kingdom. He was the head of the government and high priest of every temple. The people of Egypt considered their King to be a half-man, half-god.

The word "Pharaoh" comes from the Greek language and was used by the Greeks to refer to the Kings of Egypt. The word Pharaoh actually means "Great House", a reference to the palace where the King resided. While early Egyptians called their rulers "Kings", over time, the Greek name "Pharaoh" stuck. Today, we use the word Pharaoh when referring to the kings of Egypt. I will use both words interchangebly for the purpose of this book.

The following images carved in stone (some granite, which is one of the hardest rocks on the planet) gives us clear evidence of how the ancient egyptians represented themselves as well as their Gods.

Image 15
God Amun
Chief deity Worshipped
In ancient Egypt
The Met, New York

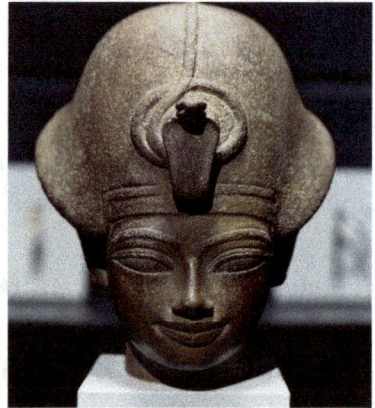

Image 16
-Pharaoh Amenhotep III-
18th Dynasty
The British Museum

Image 17
-Pharaoh Tutankhamun-
18th Dynasty
Cairo Museum, Egypt

Image 18
God Ptah
-Patron Of crafsmen and architects-
The Met, New York

Image 19
-Queen Nefertiti-
Wife of
Pharaoh Akhenaten
Cleveland Museum of Art

Image 20
-Princess Meritamun-
Daughter of Pharaoh
Ramses II aka
"Ramses The Great"

Image 21
-Queen Ahmose Nefertari-
Wife of Pharaoh Ahmose
Neues Museum, Berlin,
Germany

Image 22
-Queen Tiye-
Wife of Pharaoh
Amenhotep III
Louvre Museum, Fance

Hieroglyphs

Image 23
-Medu Neter-
Ancient writing of the
ancient Egyptians
aka Hieroglyphics

It should be noted that the people of ancient Egypt, Kemet, did not call their writing Hieroglyphics, They called it Medw Ntr pronounced "Medu Neter". It is argueably the most ancient writing system in our known historical period. Roughly, it translates as "The Writing Of The Gods", "Divine Words", "Divine Writing" or "Divine Speech". It was used on the walls of Temples, Monuments, tombs, coffins, sacred statues and papyrus scrolls.

Today, Medw Ntr, "Medu Neter", is more widely known by its Greek misnomer, "hieroglyphics" which is a word that comes from the Greek word for "sacred carving". It was first encountered in the writings of Diodorus. Other Greeks had spoken of sacred signs when referring to Egyptian writing. Diodorus also believed the ancient Egyptians learned the hieroglyhic writing from the Ethiopians.[13]

The Modern Egyptians

In recent years, there has been a shift in the media from depicting the ancient Egyptians as white Europeans to depicting them as modern day Egyptians. This representation is also factually incorrect. The look of the modern day Egyptians is the result of thousands of years

27

of invasion and migration into Egypt of Arabs, Persians and Europeans to name a few. Due to this migration, the complexion of the original Africans changed. As we will show, the lighter skinned Egyptians we see today are not a representation of the ancient native born Africans.

Keep in mind, the age of the pyramids and the Egyptian dynasties was thousands of years ago. Just as the population of the United States is not the same as it was five hundred years ago, likewise, the population of Egypt, Africa, is not the same as it was five thousand years ago.

So, again, we ask a simple question. After you finish this book, who should you believe, the people in authority, or, your lying eyes?

CHAPTER 4
The Old Kingdom/Pyramid Age

THE PHARAOHS

PHARAOH NARMER

UNITED UPPER & LOWER EGYPT - FOUNDED THE FIRST EGYPTIAN DYNASTY

Name: King Narmer

Meaning Of Name: Narmer means "painful," "stinging," "harsh," or "fierce" catfish[18]

Aka: Aha, Menes, Mena, Meni, or Min

Born: Thinnis, tjenu, southern Egypt, Africa

Years ruled: Approximately 62 years

Accomplishments: Pharaoh Narmer united Upper and Lower Egypt in approximately 3200 b.c. and founded the first Egyptian Dynasty. Before uniting Upper and Lower Egypt, he is said to have been one of the leaders of a tribal confederation in southern Egypt known as the Thinite Confederacy. After uniting Egypt, Pharaoh Narmer built a dam and founded the city of Memphis on the reclaimed land. Memphis would become the capital of Egypt during the old kingdom.[19, 21] Ptah was the chief God of ancient Memphis.[22]

Image 24
-Pharaoh Narmer-

The Petrie Museum of Egyptian Archaeology, London

Image 25
-Pharaoh Narmer-

The Narmer palette, below, is a depiction of Pharaoh Narmer conquering lower (northern) Egypt and uniting Upper and Lower Egypt.[20]

Image 26
-Narmer Palette-
Front Side
Egyptian Museum
Cairo

Image 27
-Narmer Palette-
Reverse Side
Egyptian Museum
Cairo

Once Pharaoh Narmer established himself as supreme King of Upper (southern) Egypt and Lower (northern) Egypt, he married the princess Neithhotep of Naqada in an alliance to strengthen ties between the two cities. Naqada is also located in southern Egypt. It is located further south in Egypt than Thinnis, where Pharaoh Narmer was born. Note, the ancient Egyptians did not call this land Thinnis, They called it "Tjenu". It was renamed Thinnis by the Greeks.

No images of the following pharaohs of the 1st dynasty have been located. There is a general consensus about the order of succession.

- Pharaoh Hor Aha is considered by Egyptologists to be the 2nd Pharaoh of the 1st dynasty. The number of years that he ruled is uncertain, but it is believed that he had a long reign.

- Pharaoh Djer considered by Egyptologists to be the 3rd Pharaoh of the 1st dynasty. Ruled for approximately 41 years.

- Pharaoh Djet considered by Egyptologists to be the 4th Pharaoh of the 1st dynasty. Ruled for approximately 23 years.

Pharaoh/Queen Merneith is the first documented Egyptian female ruler. She was a regent or consort for her son Den until he was mature enough to become King.

Her name is linked to the goddess Neith and means "Beloved by Neith". She ruled Egypt after the death of Den's father, Djet.

PHARAOH DEN

SON OF PHARAOH DJET

Name: King Den, 5th pharaoh of the 1st dynasty

Meaning Of Name: Den most likely meaning "He who brings the water"

Aka:

Born: Egypt, Africa

Years ruled: 42 years

Some Accomplishments: Pharaoh Den promoted the development of administration, organization, art, architecture, and religion.[23] He was also the first to use the title "King of Upper and Lower Egypt", and the first depicted as wearing the double crown of Upper and Lower Egypt (red and white crowns).[24]

Early Egyptian sources record that he fought the Bedouin tribes in Sinai and a label from Abydos shows "the first smiting of the east" (probably referring to the "smiting of the troglodytes" as recorded on the Palermo Stone.). Another label recovered from Abydos shows Den smiting an Asiatic captive.[25]

Image 28
-Pharaoh Den-
British Museum, London

Image 29
-Pharaoh Den-
British Museum, London

No images of the following Pharaohs were located.

- Pharaoh Anedjib considered by Egyptologists to be the 6th Pharaoh of the 1st dynasty. Ruled for approximately 10 years.

- Pharaoh Semerkheth considered by Egyptologists to be the 7th Pharaoh of the 1st dynasty. Ruled for approximately 9 years.

- Pharaoh Qu'a considered by Egyptlogists to be the 8th and last Pharaoh of the 1st dynasty. Ruled for approximately 33 years.

THE 2ND DYNASTY

No images were located for the following Pharaohs

- Pharaoh Hotepsekhemwy considered by Egyptologists to be the 1st Pharaoh of the 2nd dynasty. He ruled for approximately 38 years.

- Pharaoh Raneb aka Pharaoh Nebra considered by Egyptologists to be the 2nd Pharaoh of the 2nd dynasty. He ruled for approximately 39 years.

PHARAOH NYNETJER

SON OF PHARAOH NEBRA

Name: King Nynetjer, 3rd pharaoh of the 2nd dynasty

Meaning Of Name: Ninetjer means "godlike", or "He Who Belongs to the God". The term god probably in this instance references "Re", the sun god.[26]

Aka: Ninetjer and Banetjer

Born: Egypt, Africa

Years ruled: Approximately 43 years

Some Accomplishments: The Palermo stone records numerous festivals and ceremonies held during his reign.

The end of his reign seems to have been marked by poor harvests, internal tension, and possibly even civil war. The Palermo Stone records fighting in several towns including one town named "the House of the North". This reference may suggest that the king had to suppress a rebellion in Lower (northern) Egypt.[27]

*Image 30
-Pharaoh Nynetjer-
Rijksmuseum van
Oudheden, Leiden*

*Image 31
-Pharaoh Nynetjer-
Rijksmuseum van
Oudheden, Leiden*

No images were located for the following Pharaohs:

- Pharaoh Weneg aka Pharaoh considered by Egyptologists to be the 4th Pharaoh of the 2nd dynasty. Ruled for approximately 8 years.

- Pharaoh Senedj considered by Egyptologists to be the 5th Pharaoh of the 2nd dynasty. Ruled approximately for 8 years.

- Pharaoh Seth-Peribsen considered by Egyptologists to be the 6th Pharaoh of the 2nd dynasty. Ruled for approximately 17 years.

- Pharaoh Sekhemib-Perenmaat considered by Egyptologists to be the 7th Pharaoh of the 2nd dynasty. Ruled for approximately 17 years.

PHARAOH KHASEKHEMWY
THE SON OF PHARAOH SEKHEMIB-PERENMAAT

Name: King Khasekhewy, Last pharaoh of the 2nd dynasty

Meaning Of Name: Khasekhemwy means "the two powers have appeared"

Aka: Khasekhem

Born: Egypt, Africa

Years ruled: Approximately 17 years

Some Accomplishments: Pharaoh Khasekhemwy led several significant military campaigns and reunited Upper and Lower Egypt after a civil war between the followers of the gods Horus and Set. Pharaoh Khasekhemwy is unique in Egyptian history as having both the symbols of Horus and Set on his serekh. Some Egyptologists believe that this was an attempt to unify the two factions. He was the earliest Egyptian king known to have built statues of himself.[28,29]

Image 32 -Pharaoh Khasekhemwy- Oxford, Ashmolean Museum

Image 33 -Pharaoh Khasekhemwy- Oxford, Ashmolean Museum

THE 3RD DYNASTY
PHARAOH DJOSER
SON OF PHARAOH KHASEKHEWY

Name: King Djoser, 1st Pharaoh of the 3rd dynasty

Meaning Of Name:

Aka: Netjerikhet, which means "divine of body" and Zoser. The Greeks called him Tosorthros and Sesorthos

Born: Egypt, Africa

Years ruled: Approximately 29 years

Some Accomplishments: Pharaoh Djoser is credited with saving Egypt from a seven year famine by re-building the Temple of Khnum, the god of the Nile River's source.

He also brought about great technological innovations by using stone architecture to build the step pyramid at Saqqara. The Step Pyramid at Saqqara was the world's first known monumental stone building. It was designed by his architect and chief physician to the king, Imhotep, who was deified in later periods.

Pharaoh Djoser was the first pharaoh who chose to live only at Memphis rather than traveling between palaces. This made Memphis the political and cultural center of the Old Kingdom. He also extended Egypt's power all the way south to Aswan, and north to Sinai. Under Pharaoh Djosers rule, Egypt was politically and economically stable.[30, 31]

Image 34
-Pharaoh Djoser-

Image 35
-Pharaoh Djoser-
Cairo Museum
Egypt

Image 36
-Stepped Pyramid At Saqqara-
Pharaoh Djoser
Architect - Imhotep

Image 37
-Stepped Pyramid At Saqqara Recreated-
Rosenheim (Upper Bavaria). Lokschuppen
exhibition centre - "Pharao" exhibition (
2017)

The stepped pyramid of Saqqara was designed by an Egyptian named Imhotep. Imhotep means "the one who comes in peace". He is considered to be the worlds first recorded polymath (multi-genius) in history. He was an architect, an engineer, and a physician. He was also revered as a philosopher and one of only a few commoners ever to be acknowledged by the Egyptian people as having divine status after his death. Imhotep was also deified by the Greeks as Ascklepius, the god of healing.[32]

Image 38
-Imhotep-
Metropolitan Museum
Of Art
New York

Image 39
-Imhotep-
Metropolitan Museum
Of Art
New York

No images were found for the following Pharaohs:

- Pharaoh Sanakht considered by Egyptologists to be the 3rd Pharaoh of the 3rd dynasty. Ruled for approximately 18 years.

- Pharaoh Khabah considered by Egyptologists to be the 4th Pharaoh of the 3rd dynasty. Length of reign is uncertain.

PHARAOH HUNI

Lineage not confirmed

Name: King Huni, Last Pharaoh of the 3rd dynasty

Meaning Of Name:

Aka: Huni The Smiter. The Greeks called him Aches

Born: Egypt, Africa

Years ruled: Approximately 24 years

Some Accomplishments: Pharaoh Djoser may have promoted Huni to the position of pharaoh.

Next to nothing is known about the religious or military activities during his reign.

We do know that Pharaoh Huni built a fortress on the island of Elephantine to protect the border of Egypt at the First Cataract of the Nile river, near Egypts southernmost city, Aswan. He broke with tradition and built pyramids in the provinces, instead of Saqqara. He is thought to have built small step pyramids at Sinki, Ombos, Abu Rawash, Nagada, El-Kula, Edfu, and Elephantine, and may also have built a small pyramid at Zawiyet El-Meitin. .[33]

Image 40
-Pharaoh Huni-
Brooklyn Museum
New York

Image 41
-Pharaoh Huni-
Brooklyn Museum
New York

THE 4ᵀᴴ DYNASTY

PHARAOH SNEFERU

SON OF PHARAOH HUNI

Name: King Sneferu, Founder of the Fourth Dynasty

Meaning Of Name: Sneferu means "He has perfected me" or "to make beautiful"

Aka: Snefru and Snofru. The Greeks called him Soris

Born: Egypt, Africa

Years ruled: Approximately 29 years

Some Accomplishments: Pharaoh Sneferu presided over a period of expansion and technical innovation in the construction of pyramids. The three major pyramids he built were far larger than those constructed by his predecessors, and their forms illustrate the transition from the step pyramids of the 3rd dynasty to the flat-sided true pyramids built in the 4th dynasty and after.

The most well known monuments from Sneferu's reign are the three pyramids he is considered to have built in Dashur, The Bent Pyramid, The Meidum Pyramid and The Red Pyramid.[34]

Aside from the extensive import of cedar, most likely from Lebanon, there is also evidence of activity in the turquoise mines on the Sinai Peninsula during his reign.

There would also have been large-scale quarrying projects to provide Sneferu with the stone he needed for his pyramids.[35]

Image 42
-Pharaoh Sneferu-
Egyptian Museum
Cairo

Image 43
-Pharaoh Sneferu's Meidum Pyramid-

Image 44
-Pharaoh Sneferu's Bent Pyramid-

Image 45
-Pharaoh Sneferu's Red Pyramid-

PHARAOH KHUFU

SON OF PHARAOH SNEFERU

Name: King Khufu, 2nd Pharaoh of the 4th Dynasty

Meaning Of Name: Khufu's full name was Khnum-Khufwy, which means "The God Khnum protect me"

Aka: Khnum Khufu. The Greeks called him Cheops, Kheops and Suphis

Born: Egypt, Africa

Years ruled: Approximately 27- 46 years

Some Accomplishments: Pharaoh Khufu built The Great Pyramid at Giza which would be seen as the pinnacle of the Egyptian Old Kingdom's majesty and splendour, and as one of the Seven Wonders of the Ancient World.[36]

Pharaoh Khufu's pyramid is perhaps the most colossal single building ever erected on the planet. Its sides rise at an angle of 51°52' and are accurately oriented to the four cardinal points of the compass. This means each corner of The Great Pyramid is facing a different cardinal direction: North, South, East and West. The alignment at the Great Pyramid is nearly perfect, only 0.067 degrees counterclockwise from perfect cardinal alignment. This is an amazing technological accomplishment even to this day. It is the largest of the three pyramids at the Giza complex.[37]

A quick note, the Great Pyramid, unlike the other four sided pyramids at Giza, is an eight-sided structure. Each of the pyramid's four sides are evenly split from base to tip by very subtle concave indentations. These subtle lines are only visible from above, and at dawn and dusk on the spring and autumn equinoxes.[38]

Image 46
-Pharaoh Khufu-

Image 47
-Pharaoh Khufu-

Image 48
-Pharaoh Khufu's Great Pyramid at Giza-

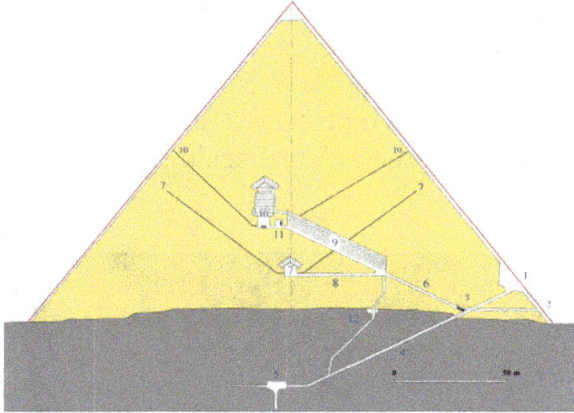

Image 49
-Pharaoh Khufu's Great
Pyramid at Giza-
Inner Structure

Image 50
-The Three Pyramids At Giza-
The "Great Pyramid" was built
by Pharaoh Khufu
The second tallest pyramid was built by
Khufu's son Khafre
The smalles of the three were built by
Khafre's son Menkaura

In addition to the Great Pyramid at Giza, Pharaoh Khufu also left behind a huge 138 feet long solar barge/solar boat. This boat is one of the oldest, largest and best-preserved vessels from antiquity. It is 43.4 metres (142 ft) long and 5.9 metres (19 ft) wide. It was identified as the world's oldest intact ship and has been described as "a masterpiece of woodcraft" that could sail today if put into a lake or a river.[39]

Image 51
-The "Khufu Ship" or " Solar Barge-
Grand Egyptian Museum (GEM)
Cairo, Egypt

Image 52
-Egyptian Sailors-
Egyptian Museum
Cairo

Image 53
-A model of The "Khufu Ship"
or " Solar Barge-
Grand Egyptian Museum (GEM)
Cairo, Egypt

Image 54
-Ancient Egyptian Sailors-
Egyptian Museum
Cairo, Egypt

PHARAOH DJEDEFRE

SON OF PHARAOH KHUFU

Name: King Djedefre, 3rd Pharaoh of the 4th Dynasty

Meaning Of Name: Djedefre means "Re is his support" or "Enduring like Re"

Aka: Djedefra. The Greeks called him Rhatoisēs

Born: Egypt, Africa

Years ruled: Approximately 10 to 14 years

Some Accomplishments: Pharaoh Djedefre is the king who introduced the royal title Sa-Rê (meaning "Son of Ra") and the first to connect his cartouche name with the sun god Ra.[40] A cartouche is an oval or oblong enclosing a group of Egyptian hieroglyphs, typically representing the name and title of the king. He also built his pyramid at Abu Rawash. Pharaoh Djedefre's pyramid was architecturally different from those of his immediate predecessors in that the chambers were beneath the pyramid instead of inside.

This allowed the chambers to be made without tunneling, and avoided the structural complications of making chambers within the body of the pyramid itself.[41, 42] Due to the poor condition of Abu Rawash, only small traces of his pyramid complex have been found.

Image 55
-Pharaoh Djedefre-

Louvre Museum
France

Image 56
-Pharaoh Djedefre-

Louvre Museum
France

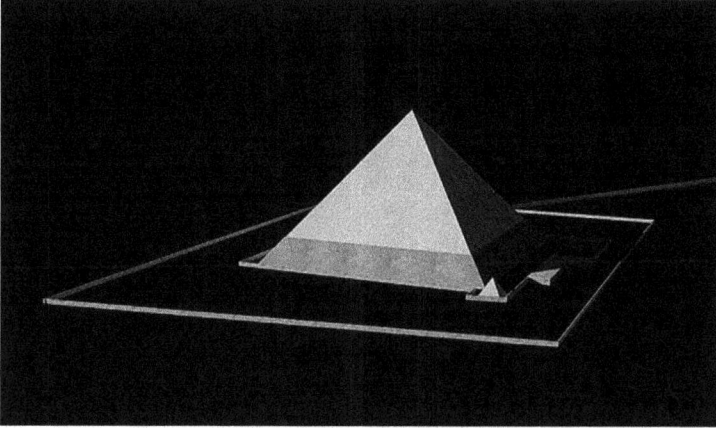

Image 57
Reconstruction of Pharaoh Djedefre's
Pyramid based on the remains

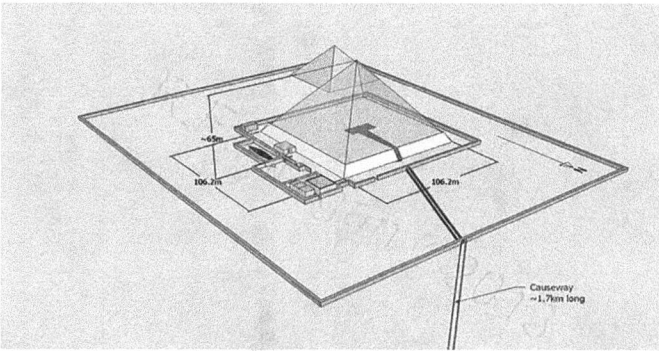

Image 58
3D Reconstruction of Pharaoh Djedefre's
Pyramid based on the remains

PHARAOH KHAFRE

SON OF PHARAOH KHUFU

Name: King khafre, 4th Pharaoh of the 4th Dynasty

Meaning Of Name: "appearing like Re"

Aka: Khafra, Sûphis II, Khêphren

Born: Egypt, Africa

Years ruled: Approximately 56 to 66 years

Some Accomplishments:. Khafre built the second largest pyramid at Giza. The Egyptian name of the pyramid was Wer(en)-Khafre which means "Khafre is Great".[43] Some people credit him as being the face of the sphinx at Giza, but that has not been confirmed.

Image 59
-Pharaoh Khafre-

Egyptian Museum Cairo

Image 60
-Pharaoh Khafre-

Egyptian Museum Cairo

Image 61
-Khafre's Pyramid &
The Great Sphinx at Giza-

PHARAOH MENKAURA
SON OF PHARAOH KHAFRE

Name: King Menkaure, 5th Pharaoh of the 4th Dynasty

Meaning Of Name: Menkaura means "Eternal like the souls of Re"

Aka: Menkaure, The Greeks called him Mykerinos or Mycerinus

Born: Egypt, Africa

Years ruled: Approximately 18 or 28 years

Some Accomplishments: According to tradition, Pharaoh Menkaura was a pious and just king. His pyramid at Giza was called Netjer-er-Menkaura, meaning "Menkaura is Divine". It was the smallest of the three main pyramids at Giza.[44, 45]

His funerary complex contained some of the finest sculptures of the Pyramid Age. They include a slate statue group of Menkaura and his sister-wife Khamerernebti II and a number of smaller slate triads representing Menkaura, the goddess Hathor and various nome (district) deities.[46]

Image 62
-Pharaoh Menkaura-

Egyptian Museum
Cairo

Image 63
-Pharaoh Menkaura-

Egyptian Museum
Cairo

Image 64
-Menkaura's Pyramid at Giza-

PHARAOH SHEPSESKAF

SON OF PHARAOH MENKAURA

Name: King Shepseskaf, Last Pharaoh of the 4th Dynasty

Meaning Of Name: Shepseskaf means "His Soul is Noble"

Aka:

Born: Egypt, Africa

Years ruled: Approximately 6 or 8 years

Some Accomplishments: Little is known about the reign of Pharaoh Shepseskaf. We do know that he completed the Pyramid of Menkaura that was started by his father Pharaoh Menkaura. Pharaoh Shepseskaf also broke with the Fourth Dynasty tradition of constructing large pyramids. It is not clear why Shepseskaf did not build a pyramid for himself.[47]

Image 65
-Pharaoh shepseskaf-

Museum Of Fine Arts
Boston

THE FIRST INTERMEDIATE PERIOD

After the Old Kingdom/Pyramid Age, Egypt experienced its first Intermediate Period.

During this time the Old Kingdom's centralized monarchy grew weak as provincial rulers called nomarchs became powerful and independent of the King/Pharaoh. The first intermediate period was a dark period in Egyptian history. Very little monumental evidence survives from this period.

The first intermediate period lasted approximately 100 to 120 years until Pharaoh Mentuhotep II, from southern Egypt, united Upper and Lower Egypt and restored stability and prosperity back to the land founding what is referred to as the Middle Kingdom or Literary Age. It was called this because art, literature and religion flourished during this period.

Pharaoh Mentuhotep II was from Thebes, "Waset" to the ancient Egyptians and is known as "Luxor" today. It is located in southern Egypt.

"Truth is a continuous examination, and fact... always supercedes belief."

- Yosef A.A. Ben-Jochannan -

CHAPTER 5
The Middle Kingdom
Literary Age

PHARAOH MENTUHOTEP II

SON OF PHARAOH INTEF III

Name: King Mentuhotep II, 5th Pharaoh of 11th Dynasty. Founded The Middle Kingdom

Meaning Of Name: Mentuhotep means "Mentu is satisfied"

Aka: Nebhepetre which means "The Lord of the rudder is Ra"

Born: Egypt, Africa

Years ruled: Approximately 50 years

Some Accomplishments: Pharaoh Mentuhotep II was the king of southern Egypt towards the end of the first intermediate period when the kings in northern Egypt threatened to invade southern Egypt. After the kings of northern Egypt desecrated the sacred ancient royal necropolis of Abydos in southern Egypt, Pharaoh Mentuhotep II dispatched his armies north to conquer northern, Egypt. His army was victorious and he reunited Upper (southern) and Lower (northern) Egypt founding the Middle Kingdom.

To reverse the decentralization of power, (which had contributed to the collapse of the Old Kingdom and started the First Intermediate Period), Pharaoh Mentuhotep II centralized the state in Thebes, Waset, as a strategy to strip monarchs of some of their power over the regions. He also created new governmental posts of Governor of Upper Egypt and Governor of Lower Egypt who had power over the local monarchs. These governors were Theban men, from southern Egypt, loyal to him, giving him more control over his country. Officials from the capital travelled the country regularly to control regional leaders. [48]

In recognition of the unification of his country, he changed his name to Shematawy meaning "He who unifies the two lands"[49, 50] Mentuhotep II returned peace and prosperity back to Egypt.[51]

Image 66
-Pharaoh Mentuhotep II-

The MET
New York

Image 67
-Pharaoh Mentuhotep II-

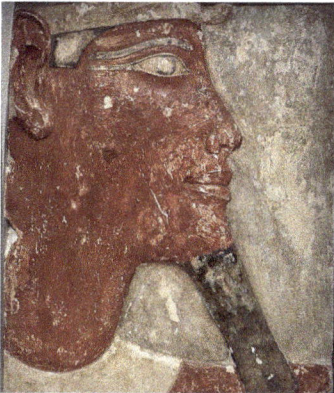

Image 68
-Pharaoh Mentuhotep II-

Rijksmuseum
van Oudheden

Image 69
-Pharaoh Mentuhotep II-

Museum Of Fine Arts
Boston

Image 70
-Pharaoh Mentuhotep II's Temple-

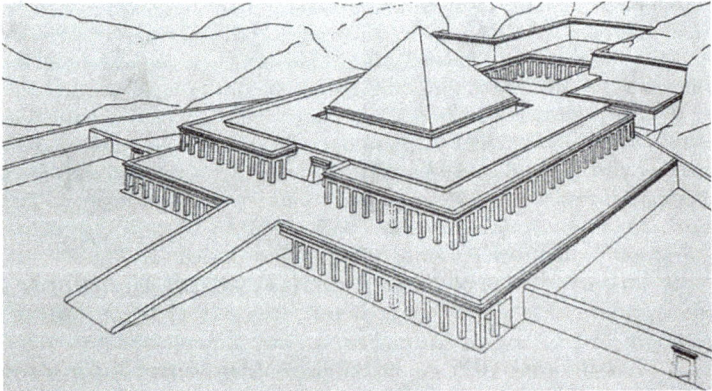

Image 71
-Pharaoh Mentuhotep II's Temple
Reconstructed-

PHARAOH MENTUHOTEP III

SON OF PHARAOH MENTUHOTEP II

Name: King Mentuhotep III, 6th Pharaoh of 11th Dynasty

Meaning Of Name: Mentuhotep means "Mentu is satisfied"

Aka:

Born: Egypt, Africa

Years ruled: Approximately 12 years

Some Accomplishments: Pharaoh Mentuhotep III sent an expedition to the Land of Punt during the 8th year of his reign, something that had not been done since the Old Kingdom. An inscription in the Wadi Hammamat describes the expedition as being 3000 men strong and under the command of the steward Henenu. As they left Coptos in the direction of the Red Sea, they dug 12 wells for future expeditions. They returned from Punt with incense, gum and perfumes, and quarried the Wadi Hammamat for stones.[52]

Image 72
-Pharaoh Mentuhotep III-

Luxor Museum
Egypt

Image 73
-Pharaoh Mentuhotep III-

Metropolitan Museum Of Art
New York

PHARAOH AMENEMHAT I

**Born to Senusret and Nefert who were
Nomarchs of one of Egypt's many provinces**

Name: King Amenemhat I, 1st   Pharaoh of 12th Dynasty

Meaning Of Name: Amenemhat means "Amun is at the Head"

Aka: He was called Ammenemes I by the Greeks

Born: Egypt, Africa

Years ruled: Approximately 28 years

Some Accomplishments: Pharaoh Amenemhet I was co-regent with his son Senusret I. He appears to have been a very wise leader who set about to correct the problems of the First Intermediate Period by protecting Egypt's borders from invasion and assuring a legitimate succession. Pharaoh Amenemhet I was murdered in an apparent harem plot while his co-regent, his son Senusret I, was leading a campaign in Libya.[53]

Image 74
-Pharaoh Amenemhat I-

*Metropolitan Museum Of
Art
New York*

Image 75
-Pharaoh Amenemhat I-

*Metropolitan Museum Of
Art
New York*

PHARAOH SENUSRET I
Son of Pharaoh Amenemhat I

Name: King Senusret I, 2nd Pharaoh of the 12th Dynasty

Meaning Of Name: Senusret means "Man of goddess Wosret"

Aka: Kheperkare. He was known as Sesostris I and Senwosret I to the Greeks

Born: Egypt, Africa

Years ruled: Approximately 45 years

Some Accomplishments: Senusret I was crowned Pharaoh after his father, Amenemhat I was assasinated.

As King, Senusret I carried on the work of his father to secure Egypts borders. He sent expeditions against the Libyans in the Western Desert and into Asia to secure the western and eastern borders of Egypt. He also expanded the borders of Egypt to the south as far as the second cataract.[54, 55]

Pharaoh Senusret I is attested to be the builder of a number of major temples in ancient Egypt, including the temple of Min at Koptos, the Temple of Satet on Elephantine, the Montu-temple at Armant and the Montu-temple at El-Tod where a long inscription of the king is preserved.[56] He also dispatched several quarrying expeditions to the Sinai and Wadi Hammamat and built numerous shrines and temples throughout Egypt and Nubia during his long reign.[57] Pharaoh Senusret I was one of the most powerful kings of the twelvth Dynasty.[58]

Image 76
-Pharaoh Senusret I-

Neues Museum
Berlin, Germany

Image 77
-Pharaoh Senusret I-

Luxor Museum
Egypt

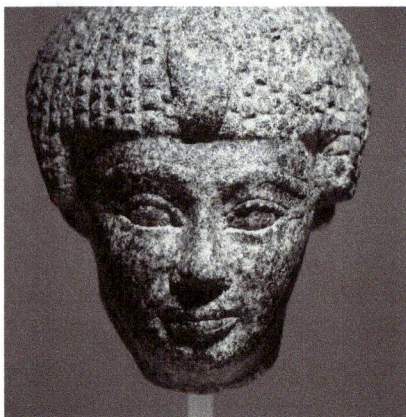

Image 78
-Pharaoh Senusret I-

Egyptian Museum
Leipzig, Germany

Image 79
-Pharaoh Senusret I-

Neues Museum
Berlin, Germany

PHARAOH AMENEMHAT II

Son of Pharaoh Senusret I

Name: King Amenemhat II, 3rd Pharaoh of 12th Dynasty

Meaning Of Name: Amenemhat means "Amun is at the Head"

Aka: He was called Amenemmes II by the Greeks

Born: Egypt, Africa

Years ruled: Approximately 35 years.

Some Accomplishments: Pharaoh Amenemhat II was co-regent with his father Senusret I. While he was coregent with his father he led a gold-mining expedition to Nubia. Later, during his own reign, more expeditions went to Nubia and Sinai for gold and copper. He also opened a new mine shaft in Sinai and a trade venture was made to Punt. Statues of Amenemhet II have been found at several Syrian cities.[59]

Image 80
-Pharaoh Amenemhat II-

Louvre Museum
France

Image 81
-Pharaoh Amenemhat II-

Louvre Museum
France

PHARAOH SENUSRET II

Son of Pharaoh <u>amenemhat II</u>

Name: King Senusret II, 4th Pharaoh of the 12th Dynasty

Meaning Of Name: Senusret means "Man of Goddess Wosret"

Aka: Kha-khaeper-re. He was known as Sesostris II and Senwosret II to the Greeks

Born: Egypt, Africa

Years ruled: Approximately 15 to 19 years

Some Accomplishments: Pharaoh Senusret II's reign ushered in a period of peace and prosperity with no recorded military campaigns and the proliferation of trade between Egypt and the Near-East.[60]

Pharaoh Senusret II took a great deal of interest in the Faiyum oasis region and began work on an extensive irrigation system from Bahr to Lake Moeris through the construction of a dike at El-Lahun and the addition of a network of drainage canals. The purpose of his project was to increase the amount of cultivable land in that area.[61]

Image 82
-Pharaoh Senusret II-

Egyptian Museum
Egypt

Image 83
-Pharaoh Senusret II-

Ny Carlsberg Glyptotek,
Copenhagen

Image 84
-Pharaoh Senusret II-

Cairo Museum
Egypt

Image 85
-Pharaoh Senusret II-

Ny Carlsberg Glyptotek,
Copenhagen

The image below, taken from the tomb painting of 12th dynasty official Khnumhotep I, shows a party of Western Asiatic foreigners visiting Pharaoh Senusret II with gifts. These foreigners are possibly Canaanites or Bedouins labelled as Aamu (ꜥ3mw).[62] Take note that the two Egyptians are darker in skin tone and dressed differently.

Image 86

-Procession Of The Aamu From The Tomb Of Khnumhotep II-

Image 87

-Procession Of The Aamu From The Tomb Of Khnumhotep II Recreated-

71

SENUSRET III
Son of Pharaoh Senusret II

Name: King Senusret III, 5ᵗʰ Pharaoh of The 12ᵗʰ Dynasty

Meaning Of Name: Senusret means "Man of goddess Wosret"

Aka: Kha-khaeper-re. He was known as Sesostris III and Senwosret III to the Greeks

Born: Egypt, Africa

Years ruled: Approximately 39 years

Some Accomplishments: Pharaoh Senusret III, was a great pharaoh and is perhaps the most powerful Egyptian ruler of the dynasty. Consequently, he is regarded as one of the sources for the legend about Sesostris. In Hertodotus' "Histories" there appears a story told by Egyptian priests about a Pharaoh Sesostris, who once led an army northward overland to Asia Minor, then fought his way westward until he crossed into Europe, where he defeated the Scythians and Thracians (possibly in modern Romania and Bulgaria). Sesostris then returned home leaving colonists behind at the river Phasis in Colchis. Herodotus cautioned the reader that much of the story came second hand via Egyptian priests, but also noted that the Colchians were commonly believed to be Egyptian colonists.[63]

His reign was characterized by military skill, decisive action, and efficient administration. He led his troops by example and always from the front. At the head of his army, he was considered invincible. His military campaigns gave rise to an era of peace and economic prosperity that reduced the power of regional rulers and led to a revival in craftwork, trade, and urban development.[64]

Pharaoh Sesostris III cut a canal through the First Nile Cataract at Elephantine, thus easing the passage of both military and commercial shipping. At the southern end of the Second Nile Cataract he also added a network of forts within signaling distance of one another, extending from the northern fort at Buhen at the

Second Nile Cataract. Nile inundation heights were also recorded at the forts giving valuable advance notice to the Pharaoh.[65]

Under Pharaoh Senusret III's rulership, the economy flourished, and military and trade expeditions filled the nation's treasury.

The Egyptians conferred upon him the rare honor of deifying him while he still lived. His followers operated at the same level and he received the same recognition as any of the great gods of Egypt.[66]

Image 88
-Pharaoh Senusret III-

The British Museum
London

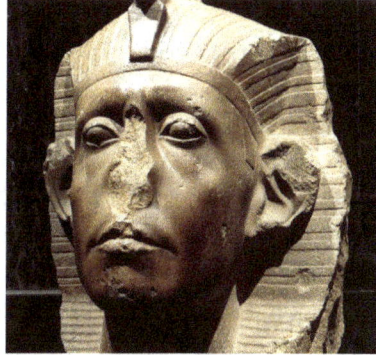

Image 89
-Pharaoh Senusret III-
Exhibit in the
Nelson-Atkins Museum of
Art, Kansas City, Missouri

Image 90
-Pharaoh Senusret III-

Munich Museum
Germany

Image 91
-Pharaoh Senusret III-
Metropolitan Museum
of Art
New York

PHARAOH AMENEMHAT III
Son of Pharaoh Senusret III

Name: King Amenemhat III, 6th Pharaoh of The 12th Dynasty

Meaning Of Name: Amenemhat means "Amun is at the Head"

Aka: The Greeks called him Amenmesses III

Born: Egypt, Africa

Years ruled: Approximately 40 years

Some Accomplishments: He was elevated to the throne as coregent by his father Senusret III with whom he shared the throne. As Pharaoh, Amenhemhat III inherited a stable and peaceful Egypt. He directed his efforts towards an extensive building program. To acquire resources for the building program, Amenemhat III exploited the quarries of Egypt and the Sinai for turquoise and copper. .[67]

Artifacts of his reign have been found from as far south as the Third Cataract of the Nile and as far northeast as Byblos which was an important seaport in Lebanon, an indication of Egypt's primacy as a commercial power. His was the last long and successful reign of the 12th dynasty.[68]

Image 92
-Pharaoh Amenemhat III-

Egyptian Museum
Cairo, Egypt

Image 93
-Pharaoh Amenemhat III-

Louvre Museum
Paris, France

PHARAOH AMENEMHAT IV
Son of Pharaoh Senusret III

Name: King Amenemhat IV, 7th Pharaoh of The 12th Dynasty

Meaning Of Name: Amenemhat means "Amun is at the Head"

Aka: The Greeks called him Amenmesses IV

Born: Egypt, Africa

Years ruled: Approximately 9 years

Some Accomplishments: He was elevated to throne as co-regent by his father Amenemhat III, with whom he shared the throne. His reign started with a seemingly peaceful two-year coregency with his father. He undertook expeditions in the Sinai for turquoise, in Upper, (southern), Egypt for amethyst, and to the Land Of Punt. He also maintained trade relations with Byblos and Nubia.[69]

Due to his fathers long reign, Amenemhet IV was old when he assumed the throne. He had no male heir and was succeeded by his sister, Neferusobek.[70]

Image 94
-Pharaoh Amenemhat III-

Metropolitan Museum Of Art
New York

Image 95
-Pharaoh Amenemhat III-

Metropolitan Museum Of Art
New York

PHARAOH/QUEEN SOBEKNEFERU

Daughter of Pharaoh Amenemhat III

Name: King Sobekneferu, last Pharaoh of The 12th Dynasty

Meaning Of Name: Sobekneferu means, "The beauties of Sobek"

Aka: Nefrusobk, Neferusobek, Sobekka

Born: Egypt, Africa

Years ruled: Approximately 4 years

Some Accomplishments: Pharaoh Sobekneferu is the first "recorded" female Pharaoh in the history of Egypt.[71] She promoted herself as king of Egypt by assuming a full royal titulary, employing kingly accoutrements, appropriating masculine garb and portraying herself in strong masculine poses. It would appear that Sobekneferu intentionally modified her attire and intensified her expression of female masculinity.[72]

Image 96
-Pharaoh Sobekneferu-

Egyptian Museum
Berlin

Image 97
-Pharaoh Sobekneferu-

Louvre Museum
France

THE SECOND INTERMEDIATE PERIOD

After the Middle Kingdom Egypt fell into disarray when it was invaded by the Hyksos , the rulers of foreign lands, who conquered most of Egypt.

The Dynasties of the Second Intermediate Period included The Twelfth Dynasty, the Thirteenth Dynasty, the Fourteenth Dynasty, the Fifteenth Dynasty, the Sixteenth Dynasty and the Seventeenth Dynasty.

Once again, it was a king from southern Egypt named Ahmose I who expelled the foreigners from Egypt uniting Upper (southern) Egypt and Lower (northern) Egypt Founding the New Kingdom. He also reestablished the ancient Egyptian customs.

"I saw no African people in the printed and illustrated sunday school lessons. I began to suspect at this early age that someone had distorted the image of my people. My long search for the true history of African people the world over began."

- Dr. John Henrik Clarke -

CHAPTER 6
The New Kingdom

PHARAOH AHMOSE I

Son of Pharaoh Seqenenre Tao

Name: King Ahmose I, 1ˢᵗ Pharaoh of The 18ᵗʰ Dynasty. Founder of The New Kingdom

Meaning Of Name: Ahmose means "Iah (The Moon) is born"

Aka: Amosis and Aahmes. The Greeks called him Amasis

Born: Egypt, Africa

Years ruled: Approximately 25 years

Some Accomplishments: Pharaoh Ahmose I was from Thebes, Waset, southern Egypt, and a member of the Theban Royal House. During his reign, Ahmose I completed the conquest and expulsion of the Hyksos from Egypt and restored Theban rule over the whole of Egypt.[73]

He reorganized the administration of the country, reopened quarries, mines and trade routes. He also began massive construction projects of a type that had not been undertaken since the time of the Middle Kingdom. This building program culminated in the construction of the last pyramid built by native Egyptian rulers.[74]

With the re-unification of Upper and Lower Egypt under Pharaoh Ahmose I, a renewal of royal support for the arts and monumental construction occurred. He reportedly devoted a tenth of all the productive output towards the service of the traditional Gods.[75]

Ahmose I's reign laid the foundations for the New Kingdom under which Egyptian power reached its peak.

Image 98
-Pharaoh Ahmose I-
Metropolitan Museum
Of Art
New York

Image 99
-Pharaoh Ahmose I-
Metropolitan Museum
Of Art
New York

Image 100
-Pharaoh Ahmose I-

Louvre Museum
France

Image 101
-Pharaoh Ahmose I-

Metropolitan Museum
Of Art
New York

PHARAOH AMENHOTEP I

Son of Pharaoh Ahmose I

Name: King Amenhotep I, 2nd Pharaoh of The 18th Dynasty

Meaning Of Name: Amenhotep means "Amun is satisfied"

Aka: Djeserkere. The Greeks called him Amenophis I or Amenôthes I

Born: Egypt, Africa

Years ruled: Approximately 20 years

Some Accomplishments: Because of the numerous years of peace during Amenhotep I's reign, he embarked on various elaborate building projects and repaired and restored many ancient temples along the Nile. He also restored the mines at Serabit el-Khadim in the Sinai where he also expanded the Middle Kingdom temple of Hathor.[76]

Image 102
-Pharaoh Amenhotep I-

Egyptian antiquities
in Museo
Barracco, Rome

Image 103
-Pharaoh Amenhotep I-

Metropolitan Museum
Of Art
New York

PHARAOH THUTHMOSE I

Son of Pharaoh Amenhotep I

Name: King Thuthmose I, 3rd Pharaoh of The 18th Dynasty

Meaning Of Name: Thuthmose I means "Thoth is born"

Aka: Thuthmosis I

Born: Egypt, Africa

Years ruled: Disputed

Some Accomplishments: During his reign, Pharaoh Thuthmose I expanded Egypt's empire in Nubia, present-day Sudan, and also penetrated deep into Syria.[77]

He also built many temples in Egypt, and a tomb for himself in the Valley of the Kings. He is the first king confirmed to have done this (although Pharaoh Amenhotep I may have preceded him).[78]

Image 104
-Pharaoh Thuthmose I-

Egyptian Museum
Cairo

Image 105
-Pharaoh Thuthmose I-

The British Museum
London

Image 106
-Pharaoh Thuthmose I-

Egyptian Museum
Cairo

Image 107
-Pharaoh Thuthmose I-

Egyptian Museum
Cairo

Image 108
-Scene of a statue of Thutmose I, he
is depicted in the symbolic black
color of deification, the black color
also symbolizes rebirth
and regeneration-

Metropolitan Museum Of Art
New York

PHARAOH THUTHMOSE II

Son of Pharaoh Thuthmose I

Name: King Thuthmose II, 4th   Pharaoh of The 18th Dynasty

Meaning Of Name: Thuthmose means "Thoth is born"

Aka: Djehutymes. The Greeks called him Thothmes & Thuthmosis

Born: Egypt, Africa

Years ruled: Approximately 13 years

Some Accomplishments: Thutmose II chose to marry his fully royal half-sister, Hatshephut, in order to secure his kingship. As pharaoh he managed to stop a rebellion in Kush by sending an army to Nubia. His armies also crushed rebellions in the Levant, historic Palestine, Israel and Syria. They also defeated a group of nomadic Bedouins in the Sinai Peninsula. Even though Thutmose II did not lead these campaigns himself, he is credited with the results. The armies were, in fact, led by the king's generals. Some archaeologists believe that Hatshepsut was the real power behind the throne during the early rule of Pharaoh Thutmose II.[79]

No images were located of Pharaoh Thuthmose II.

PHARAOH/QUEEN HATSHEPHUT

Daughter of Pharaoh Thuthmose I

Name: King Hatshephut, 5th Pharaoh of The 18th Dynasty

Meaning Of Name: Hatshephut means "Foremost of Noble Ladies"

Aka: Hatchepsut

Born: Egypt, Africa

Years ruled: Approximately 21 years

Some Accomplishments: Pharaoh Hatshephut was the second historically confirmed female pharaoh and by far the most successful. She re-established the trade networks that had been disrupted during the Hyksos occupation of Egypt during the Second Intermediate Period thereby building the wealth of the Eighteenth Dynasty. She also funded a trip to the Land Of Punt.[80]

*Image 109
-Pharaoh/Queen
Hatshephut-*

*Metropolitan Museum
Of Art
New York*

*Image 110
-Pharaoh/Queen
Hatshephut-*

*Metropolitan Museum
Of Art
New York*

Image 111
-Pharaoh/Queen
Hatshephut-

Metropolitan Museum
Of Art
New York

Image 112
-Pharaoh/Queen
Hatshephut-

Metropolitan Museum
Of Art
New York

Image 113
-Pharaoh/Queen
Hatshephut-

Metropolitan Museum
Of Art
New York

Image 114
-Pharaoh/Queen
Hatshephut-

Museum Of Fine Arts
Boston

Image 115
-Temple Of Hatshephut-
Deir el-Bahari, Luxor, Egypt

Image 116
-Temple Of Hatshephut-
Deir el-Bahari, Luxor, Egypt

Image 117
-Temple Of Hatshephut-
Deir el-Bahari, Luxor, Egypt

Image 118
-Temple Of Hatshephut-
Deir el-Bahari, Luxor, Egypt

PHARAOH THUTHMOSE III

Son of Pharaoh Thuthmose II

Name: King Thuthmose III, 6th Pharaoh of The 18th Dynasty

Meaning Of Name: Thuthmose means "Thoth is born"

Aka: Thuthmose The Conqueror, Thuthmosis

Born: Egypt, Africa

Years ruled: Approximately 54 years

Some Accomplishments: Pharaoh Thuthmose III is widely considered a military genius by historians.[81]

He created the largest empire Egypt had ever seen. No fewer than 17 campaigns were conducted as he conquered lands from the Niya Kingdom in northern Syria to the fourth cataract of the Nile river in Nubia, ancient kingdom of Kush, modern day Sudan.[82]

He was an active expansionist ruler called Egypt's greatest conqueror or "the Napoleon of Egypt" by the Egyptologist James Breasted.[83, 84]

Pharaoh Thuthmose III brought the Egyptian empire to the zenith of its power by conquering all of Syria, crossing the Euphrates river to defeat the Mitannians, and penetrating south along the Nile River to Napata in modern day Sudan. He also built a great number of temples and monuments to commemorate his deeds.[85]

The annals and conquests of this military genius are far too numerous to list here. Please conduct your own research. To give you an idea, a map of the Egyptian Empire during the reign of Pharaoh Thuthmose III is provided.

Image 119
-Pharaoh Thuthmose III-
Thuthmosis The Conqueror
Louvre Museum
France

Image 120
-Ancient Egyptian Empire
Under Thutmose III-

Image 121
-Pharaoh Thuthmose III-
Kunsthistorisches
Museumin
Vienna

Image 122
-Pharaoh Thuthmose III-
Thuthmosis The Conqueror
Luxor Museum
Egypt

91

PHARAOH AMENHOTEP II

Son of Pharaoh Thuthmose III

Name: King Amenhotep II, 7th Pharaoh of The 18th Dynasty

Meaning Of Name: Amenhotep means "Amun is satisfied"

Aka: Djeserkere. The Greeks called him Amenophis II or Amenôthes II

Born: Egypt, Africa

Years ruled: Uncertain

Some Accomplishments: Pharaoh Amenhotep II inherited a vast kingdom from his father Thuthmosis III, and held it by means of a few military campaigns in Syria. He fought much less than his father and his reign saw the effective cessation of hostilities between Egypt and Mitanni, the major kingdoms vying for power in Syria.[86]

*Image 123
-Pharaoh Amenhotep II-*

*Ny Carlsberg Glyptotek,
Copenhagen*

*Image 124
-Pharaoh Amenhotep II-
Staatliches Museum
Ägyptischer Kunst
München*

Image 125
-Pharaoh Amenhotep II-

Ny Carlsberg Glyptotek,
Copenhagen

Image 126
-Pharaoh Amenhotep II-
Staatliches Museum
Ägyptischer Kunst
Munich

Image 127
-Pharaoh Amenhotep II-

The Egyptian Museum
Berlin, Germany

Image 128
-Pharaoh Amenhotep II-
The Metropolitan
Museum Of Art
New York

PHARAOH THUTHMOSE IV

Son of Pharaoh Amenhotep II

Name: King Thuthmose IV, 6th   Pharaoh of The 18th Dynasty

Meaning Of Name: Thuthmose means "Thoth is born"

Aka: Thuthmosis

Born: Egypt, Africa

Years ruled: Approximately 10 years

Some Accomplishments: As prince, Thutmose was assigned to the military operational base at Memphis.   During a rest near the great Sphinx, he dreamed that the god Horus, whom the sphinx was believed to represent, asked him to free it of sand that had drifted around it. In return, he would become pharaoh. On the basis of this dream, it has been suggested that Thutmose was not the heir apparent and that he succeeded after an elder brother's death, using the dream as divine sanction of his rule.[87]

As king, Thutmose IV made an armed tour of Syria-Palestine, during which he quelled some minor uprisings. Sensing the growing menace of the Hittite empire in Asia Minor, he initiated lengthy negotiations with the Mitanni empire, Egypt's former foe in Syria, which culminated in a peace treaty between the two powers, cemented by a royal marriage between a Mitanni princess and Pharaoh Thuthmosis IV. Gifts were exchanged, and the city of Alalakh, present-day Açana in southern Turkey, was ceded to Mitanni. A long peace marked by friendly relations ensued between the two states.During the remainder of his peaceful reign, Thutmose IV erected an obelisk that was the tallest obelisk ever erected in Egypt. It was called tekhen waty or "unique obelisk". It was transported to the grounds of the Circus Maximus in Rome by Emperor Constantius II in 357 AD and, later, "re-erected by Pope Sixtus V at the Piazza San Giovanni" before the church of St. John Lateran in Rome where   it is today known as the Lateran Obelisk.[89]

Image 129
-Pharaoh Thuthmose IV-

State Museum of
Egyptian Art
Munich, Germany

Image 130
-Pharaoh Thuthmose IV-

Louvre Museum
France

Image 131
-Thuthmose IV & Anubis-

Tomb Of Thuthmose IV
Valley of the Kings,
Luxor, Egypt

PHARAOH AMENHOTEP III

Son of Pharaoh Thuthmose IV

Name: King Amenhotep III, 9th Pharaoh of The 18th Dynasty

Meaning Of Name: Amenhotep means "Amun is satisfied"

Aka: Amenhotep the Magnificent or Amenhotep the Great. The Greeks called him Amenophis III or Amenôthes III

Born: Egypt, Africa

Years ruled: Approximately 30 years

Some Accomplishments: His reign was a period of unprecedented prosperity and splendour, when Egypt reached the peak of its artistic and international power.[90]

In this period of peaceful prosperity, he devoted himself to expanding diplomatic contacts and to extensive building in Egypt and Nubia. His Great Royal Wife was Queen Tiye.[91]

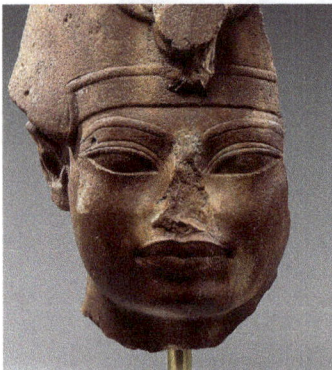

Image 132
-Pharaoh Amenhotep III-

*Metropolitan Museum
Of Art
New York*

Image 133
-Pharaoh Amenhotep III-

Image 134
-Pharaoh Amenhotep III-

Metropolitan Museum
Of Art
New York

Image 135
-Pharaoh Amenhotep III-

Rijksmuseum van
Ouheden, Leiden

Image 136
-Pharaoh Amenhotep III-

Pergamon Museum,
Berlin

Image 137
-Pharaoh Amenhotep III-

British Museum
London

Image 138
-Queen Tiye-
Wife of Pharaoh
Amenhotep III
Louvre Museum, France

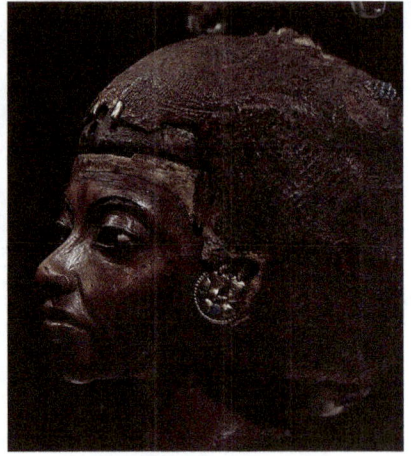

Image 139
-Queen Tiye-
Wife of Pharaoh
Amenhotep III
Louvre Museum, France

Image 140
-Queen Tiye-
Wife of Pharaoh
Amenhotep III
Neues Museum, Berlin,
Germany

Image 141
-Queen Tiye-
Wife of Pharaoh
Amenhotep III

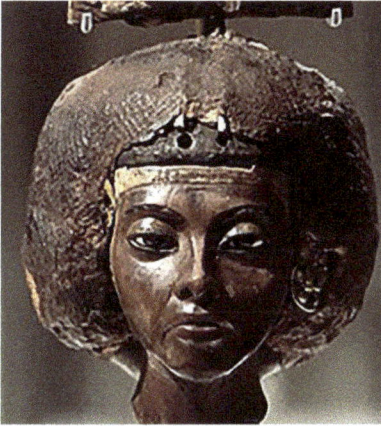

Image 142
-Queen Tiye-
Wife of Pharaoh
Amenhotep III
Neues Museum
Berlin, Germany

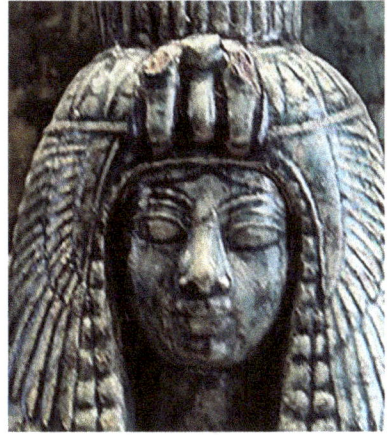

Image 143
-Queen Tiye-
Wife of Pharaoh
Amenhotep III
Louvre Museum
France

PHARAOH AKHENATEN

Son of Pharaoh Amenhotep III

Name: King Akhenaten, 10th Pharaoh of The 18th Dynasty

Meaning Of Name: Akhenaton, means "the Servant of Aten"

Aka: Amenhotep IV, Amenophis IV

Born: Egypt, Africa

Years ruled: Approximately 20 years

Some Accomplishments: As a pharaoh, Akhenaten is noted for abandoning Egypt's traditional polytheism and introducing Atenism, or worship centered around Aten. This culture shift away from traditional religion was not widely accepted.

Before the fifth year of his reign, he was known as Amenhotep IV.[92]

In the fifth year of his reign, He changed his name from Amenhotep ("Amon Is Satisfied") to Akhenaten ("Beneficial to Aton"). His Great Royal Wife was Queen Nefertiti. Nefertiti means, "The Beautiful One Has Arrived". Her name was expanded to Neferneferuaten (Beautiful Is the Beauty of Aton) – Nefertiti.

Akhenaten moved his capital to a new site some 200 miles (300 km) north of Thebes. The location chosen for the new capital, named Akhetaton ("Horizon of the Aton"; Tell el-Armana) was a virgin site on the east bank of the Nile River.[9]

Traditional religious practices were gradually restored, after Akhenatens son and successor Tutankhamun became Pharaoh. His name was originally Tutankhaten but he changed it to Tutankhamun early in his reign.[94]

Image 144
-Pharaoh Akhenaten-

Altes Museum
Berlin

Image 145
-Pharaoh Akhenaten-

Tutankhamun Exhibition,
Seattle, WA

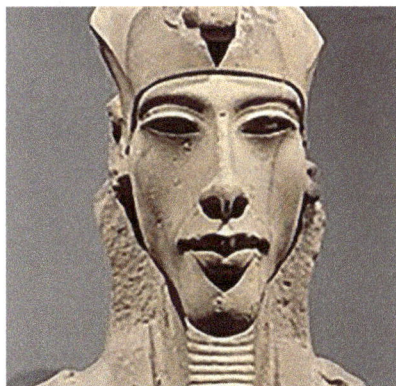

Image 146
-Pharaoh Akhenaten-

Luxor Museum
Egypt

Image 147
-Pharaoh Akhenaten-

Metropolitan Museum
Of Art
New York

Image 148
-Pharaoh Akhenaten-

Cleveland Museum
of Art
Cleveland, Ohio

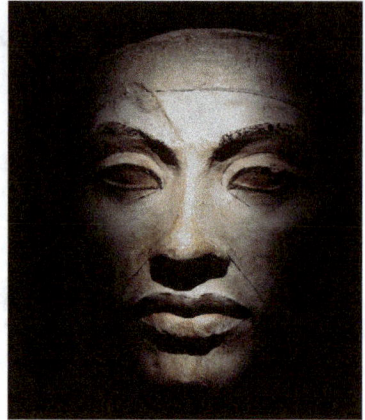

Image 149
-Pharaoh Akhenaten-

Egyptian Museum
Cairo

Image 150
-Queen Nefertiti-
Wife of
Pharaoh Akhenaten
Cleveland Museum
of Art

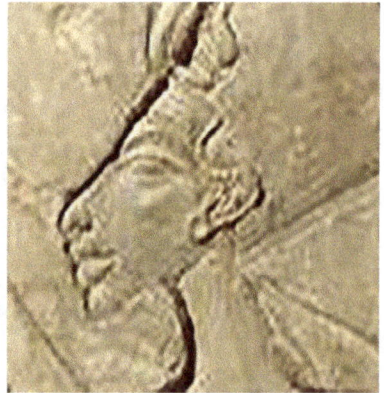

Image 151
-Queen Nefertiti-
Wife of
Pharaoh Akhenaten
Ashmolean Museum
Oxford, England

Image 152
-Queen Nefertiti-
Wife of
Pharaoh Akhenaten
Neues Museum
Berlin

Image 153
-Queen Nefertiti-
Wife of
Pharaoh Akhenaten
Metropolitan Museum
Of Art
New York

Image 154
-Queen Nefertiti-
Wife of
Pharaoh Akhenaten
Brooklyn Museum
New York

Image 155
-Queen Nefertiti-
Wife of
Pharaoh Akhenaten
Neues Museum
Berlin

Image 156
- Relief of Akhenaten, Nefertiti
and two daughters adoring
the Aten-
Cairo Museum
Egypt

Image 157
-Akhenaten, Nefertiti
and their children-

Egyptian Museum Of Berlin
Germany

PHARAOH SMENKHKARE

Lineage unknown

Name: King Smenkhkare, 11th   Pharaoh of The 18th   Dynasty

Meaning Of Name: Smenkhkare means "'Vigorous is the Soul of Re"

Aka: The romans called him Smenkare, or Smenkhkaa

Born: Egypt, Africa

Years ruled: Unconfirmed

Some Accomplishments: Very little is known of Pharaoh Smenkhkare because later kings sought to erase the Amarna Period from history. He was the husband of Queen Meritaten who was one of Pharaoh Akhenatens six daughters.   No images of Pharaoh Smenkhare were located.   Below are images of his wife Queen Meritaten.

Image 158
-Queen Meritaten-
Wife of
Pharaoh Smenkhkare
Louvre Museum
France

Image 159
-Queen Meritaten-
Wife of
Pharaoh Smenkhkare
Brooklyn Museum
New York

PHARAOH TUTANKHAMUN

Son of Pharaoh Akhenaten

Name: King Tutankhamun, 12th Pharaoh of The 18th Dynasty

Meaning Of Name: Tutankhamun means "Living image of Amun"

Aka: Tutankhaten which means "Living image of Aten", King Tut

Born: Egypt, Africa

Years ruled: Approximately 9 years

Some Accomplishments: Tutankhamun took the throne at eight or nine years of age under the unprecedented viziership of his eventual successor, Ay. Tutankhamun restored the Ancient Egyptian religion after its dissolution by his father, enriched and endowed the priestly orders of two important cults and began restoring old monuments damaged during the previous Amarna period. He also relocated the capital of Egypt from Akhenaten back to Thebes. [95]

Image 160
-Pharaoh Tutankhamun-

Cairo Museum
Egypt

Image 161
-Pharaoh Tutankhamun-

Museum Of Fine Arts
Boston

Image 162
-Pharaoh Tutankhamun-

Egyptian Museum
Cairo

Image 163
-Pharaoh Tutankhamun-

Cairo Museum
Egypt

Image 164
-Pharaoh Tutankhamun-

Treasure of Tutankhamun,
exposition in Paris 2012

Image 165
-Pharaoh Tutankhamun-

Cairo Museum
Egypt

Image 166
-Tutankhamun embraces Osiris-

Taken From His Tomb
Valley Of The Kings

Image 167
-Pharaoh Tutankhamun & his wife
Ankhesenamun-

Taken From His Tomb
Valley Of The Kings

PHARAOH AYE

Lineage unknown

Name: King Aye, 13th Pharaoh of The 18th Dynasty

Meaning Of Name: Ay means "Father Of God"

Aka:

Born: Egypt, Africa

Years ruled: Approximately 4 years

Some Accomplishments: He rose from the ranks of the civil service and the military to become king after the death of Pharaoh Tutankhamun. Prior to his rule, he was a close advisor to two, and perhaps three, other pharaohs of the dynasty. It is theorized that he was the power behind the throne during Tutankhamun's reign.[96]

Image 168
-Pharaoh Ay-

Tomb of Ay
El-Amarna, Egypt

Image 169
-Pharaoh Ay-
Wall Painting
from Tutankhamun's
tomb-
Valley Of The Kings
Egypt

PHARAOH HOREMHEB

Lineage unknown

Name: King Horemheb, Last Pharaoh of The 18th Dynasty

Meaning Of Name: Horemhab means, "Horus is in Festival"

Aka: Dejserkheprure, Horemhab or Haremhab

Born: Egypt, Africa

Years ruled: Approximately 14 years

Some Accomplishments: Before he became pharaoh, Horemheb was the commander in chief of the army under the reigns of Tutankhamun and Ay. He ruled for approximately 14 years.[97]

He had no heir to take the throne and so appointed his vizier and former comrade-in-arms Paramesse as heir to the throne. Paramesse took the name Rameses I upon his ascension and founded the 19th dynasty of Egypt.[98]

Image 170
-Pharaoh Horemheb-
Wall Painting
from Tomb Of Horemheb
Valley Of The Kings
Egypt

Image 171
-Pharaoh Horemheb-

Luxor Museum
Egypt

THE 19TH DYNASTY

PHARAOH RAMSES I
Son of a troop commander called Seti

Name: King Ramses I, 1st Pharaoh of The 19th Dynasty

Meaning Of Name: Ramses means "Ra bore him"

Aka:

Born: Egypt, Africa

Years ruled: Approximately 1 year

Some Accomplishments: Ramses I descended from a nonroyal military family. He found favour with Horemheb the last king of the 18th dynasty who was also a military man. As the elderly king had no son of his own, he made Ramses coregent not long before his own death. By then Ramses also was of advanced age, but his son Seti was in the prime of life.[99]

Image 172
-Pharaoh Ramses I-
Staatliches Museum
Ägyptischer Kunst
Munich

Image 173
-Pharaoh Ramses I-

Museum Of Fine Arts
Boston

PHARAOH SETI I

Son of Pharaoh Ramses I

Name: King Seti I, 2ⁿᵈ Pharaoh of The 19ᵗʰ Dynasty

Meaning Of Name: Seti means "Of Set"

Aka: The Greeks called him Sethos I

Born: Egypt, Africa

Years ruled: Approximately 11 to 15 years

Some Accomplishments: After the enormous social upheavals generated by Pharaoh Akhenaten's religious reform, Pharaoh Horemheb, Ramses and Seti I's main priority was to re-establish order in the kingdom and to reaffirm Egypt's sovereignty over Canaan and Syria, which had been compromised by the increasing external pressures from the Hittite States.[100]

Pharaoh Seti I led his army northward to restore Egyptian prestige, which had been partly lost during the troubled years of the late 18ᵗʰ dynasty. He battled in northern Palestine and Syria and fought at least one battle with the Hittite king Muwatallis; he subsequently concluded a peace treaty that may have established the frontier at Kadesh on the Orontes River between the Lebanon and Anti-Lebanon mountains.

He fortified the frontier, opened mines and quarries, dug wells, and rebuilt temples and shrines that had fallen into decay or been damaged. He also continued the work begun by his father on the construction of the great hypostyle hall at Karnak. which is one of the most impressive monuments of Egyptian architecture.[101]

Image 174
-Pharaoh Seti I-

Image 175
-Pharaoh Seti I-

Seti I Temple Relief at
Abydos, Egypt

Louvre Museum
France

Image 176
-Pharaoh Seti I before Thot-

tomb of Pharaoh Seti I
Valley Of The Kings
Egypt

PHARAOH RAMSES II

Son of Pharaoh Seti *I*

Name: King Ramses II, 3rd Pharaoh of The 19th Dynasty.

Meaning Of Name: Ramses means "Ra bore him"

Aka: Pa-ra-mes-su, "Ramses The Great", The Great Ancestor, Ramessu or Ramesses

Born: Egypt, Africa

Years ruled: Approximately 66 years

Some Accomplishments: Pharaoh Ramses II is often regarded as the greatest, most celebrated, and most powerful pharaoh of the New Kingdom. The early part of his reign was focused on building cities, temples, and monuments. He established the city of Pi- Ramesses in the Nile Delta as his new capital and used it as the main base for his campaigns in Syria. He led several military expeditions into the Levant, (Syria, Lebanon Jordan, Israel, Palestine and most of Turkey) reasserting Egyptian control over Canaan.[102]

The battle of Kadesh against the Hittites is legendary and should be researched independently.   Fifteen years after the battle, the Egyptians and Hittites signed a treaty to end the long war between the two groups. Known as the Eternal Treaty (or the Treaty of Kadesh), this agreement is the first of its kind in history, with surviving documents from both sides.[103]

In Nubia,(modern day Sudan), Pharaoh Ramses II constructed no fewer than six temples. The most famous of these temples are two which are carved out of a cliffside at Abu Simbel that have four colossal statues of the king.[104]

Image 177
-Pharaoh Ramses II-
Ramses The Great
Egyptian Museum
Cairo, Egypt

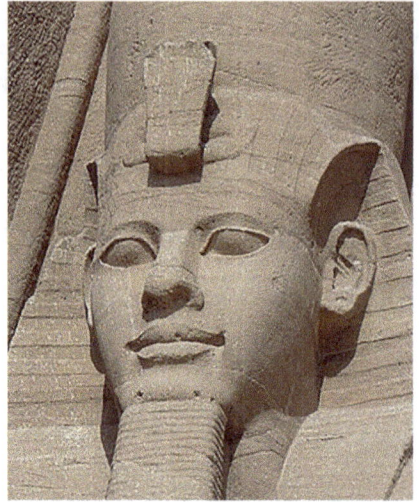

Image 178
-Pharaoh Ramses II-
Ramses The Great
Great Temple of
Ramesses II
Abu Simbel
Egypt

Image 179
-Pharaoh Ramses II-
Ramses The Great
Manchester Museum,
Manchester,
Kingdom.

Image 180
-Pharaoh Ramses II-
Ramses The Great
University Museum
Strasbourg, France

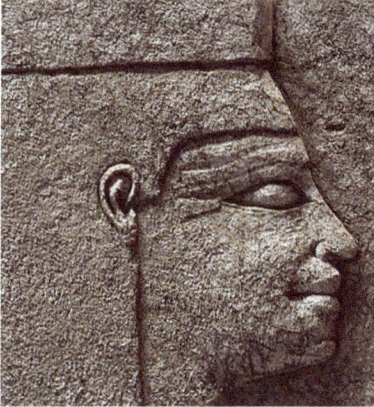

Image 181
-Queen Ahmose Nefertari-
Wife Of Pharaoh Ramses II
"The Great"

Louvre Museum
France

Image 182
-Queen Ahmose Nefertari-
Wife Of Pharaoh Ramses II
"The Great"
Deified Queen
Ahmose-Nefertari
Neues Museum
Berlin

Image 183
-Queen Ahmose Nefertari-
Wife Of Pharaoh Ramses II
"The Great"

Neues Museum
Berlin

Image 184
-Queen Ahmose Nefertari-
Wife Of Pharaoh Ramses II
"The Great"

Egyptian Museum
Italy

Image 185
-Queen Ahmose Nefertari
Playing Senet-

Metropolitan Museum
Of Art
New York

Image 186
-Temple of Ramesses II-

Abu Simbel
Southern, Egypt

Image 187
-Temple of Ramesses II-

Abu Simbel
Southern, Egypt

Image 188
-Temple Of Hathor
& Queen Nefertari-
Hathor Was The Goddess
Of Love & Music

Image 189
-Temple Of Hathor
& Queen Nefertari-
Hathor Was The Goddess
Of Love & Music

PHARAOH MERNEPTAH

Son of Pharaoh Ramses II

Name: King Merneptah, 4th Pharaoh of The 19th Dynasty

Meaning Of Name: Merneptah means "Beloved of Ptah, Joyous is Truth"

Aka: Merenptah

Born: Egypt, Africa

Years ruled: Approximately 10 years

Some Accomplishments: Pharaoh Merneptah carried out several military campaigns during his reign. In the fifth year of his rule, he fought against the Libyans, who, with the assistance of the Sea Peoples, were threatening Egypt from the west. Merneptah led a victorious six-hour battle against a combined Libyan and Sea People force at the city of Perire, probably located on the western edge of the Nile Delta. He also moved the administrative center of Egypt from his father's capital, Piramesse (Pi-Ramesses), back to Memphis where he constructed a royal palace next to the temple of Ptah.[105]

Image 190
-Pharaoh Merneptah-

Thorvaldsens Museum,
Copenhagen, Denmark

Image 191
-Pharaoh Merenptah-

Metropolitan Museum
Of Art
New York

PHARAOH SETI II

Son of Pharaoh Merneptah

Name: King Seti II , 5th Pharaoh of The 19th Dynasty

Meaning Of Name: His throne name Userkheperure Setepenre, means "Powerful are the manifestations of Re" or, "The chosen one of Re."[106]

Aka: "Sethos II" to the Greeks

Born: Egypt, Africa

Years ruled: Approximately 6 years

Some Accomplishments: Pharaoh Seti II sat on the throne during a period known for dynastic intrigue and short reigns, and his reign was no different. Seti II had to deal with many serious plots; most significantly the accession of a rival king named Amenmesse who was possibly his half brother, who had seized control over Thebes and Nubia in Upper, (southern), Egypt during his second to fourth years of his reign.[107]

Image 192
-Pharaoh Seti II-

Museo Egizio,
Turin, Italy

Image 193
-Pharaoh Seti II-

Metropolitan Museum
Of Art
New York

PHARAOH AMENMESSE

Son of Pharaoh Merneptah or Ramses II

Name: King Amenmesse, 3rd   Pharaoh of The 19th Dynasty

Meaning Of Name: Amenmesse means "born of or fashioned by Amun"

Aka: Amenmesses or Amenmose

Born: Egypt, Africa

Years ruled: Approximately 4 years

Some Accomplishments: Not much is known about this Pharaohs short reign. Amenmesse somehow managed to usurp the throne at Thebes and parts of Upper, (southern), Egypt from Pharaoh Seti II, who was possibly his half brother. His reign only lasted a year or two before he was ousted and presumably killed.[108, 109]

Image 194
-Pharaoh Amenmesse-

Louvre Museun
France

PHARAOH SIPTAH

Possible Pharaoh Seti II or Pharaoh Amenmesse

Name: King Siptah, 3rd Pharaoh of The 19th Dynasty

Meaning Of Name:

Aka: Akhenre Setepenre Siptah or Merenptah Siptah

Born: Egypt, Africa

Years ruled: Approximately 6 years

Some Accomplishments: Not much is known about the reign of Pharaoh Siptah. His father's identity is currently unknown. Both Seti II and Amenmesse have been suggested although the fact that Siptah later changed his royal name or nomen to Merneptah Siptah suggests that his father was Merneptah.[110]

Image 195
-Pharaoh Siptah-

Siptah's tomb,
Valley of Kings
Egypt

Image 196
-Pharaoh Siptah-

Egypt

PHARAOH/QUEEN TWOSRET

Daughter of Pharaoh Merenptah

Name: King Twosret , Last   Pharaoh of The 19th Dynasty

Meaning Of Name:

Aka: Tawosret or Tausret

Years ruled: Approximately 3 years

Some Accomplishments: Pharaoh/Queen Twosret was the last ruler of the New Kingdom and one of the few women to rule ancient Egypt as a king with full pharaonic honours.

The Greek poet Homer made reference to a king, Polybus, and his wife, Alcandra, who ruled Egypt during the Trojan War. Manetho recorded that the name of Polybus was in fact Thuoris, and "he" was the ruler of Egypt when Troy fell. It is now generally agreed that Manetho got the gender of the king wrong - Thuoris was actually Queen Twosret.[111]

Image 197
-Pharaoh Twosret-
holding two sistrums-

Amada Temple
Nubia

PHARAOH SETNAKHTE

Lineage unsure

Name: King Setnakhte , 1st Pharaoh of The 20th Dynasty

Meaning Of Name:

Aka: Setnakht or Sethnakht

Born: Egypt, Africa

Years ruled: Approximately 3 years

Some Accomplishments: While Setnakhte's reign was comparatively brief, it was just long enough for him to stabilize the political situation in Egypt and establish his son, Rameses III, as his successor to the throne of Egypt.[112]

Image 198
-Pharaoh Setnakhte-

Metropolitan Museum
Of Art
New York

Image 199
-Pharaoh Setnakhte-

Drawing of a relief of
pharaoh Sethnakht

PHARAOH RAMSES III

Son of Pharaoh Setnakhte

Name: King Ramses III, 2nd Pharaoh of The 20th Dynasty

Meaning Of Name: Ramses means "Ra bore him"

Aka: Ramesses

Born: Egypt, Africa

Years ruled: Approximately 32 years

Some Accomplishments: Pharaoh Ramses III's long reign saw the decline of Egyptian political and economic power, linked to a series of invasions and internal economic problems that also plagued pharaohs before him.

He led the way by defeating the invaders, known as "the Sea Peoples", who had caused destruction in other civilizations and empires. He was able to save Egypt from collapsing at the time when many other empires fell during the Late Bronze Age. However, the damage of the invasions took a toll on Egypt.[113] These economic difficulties and internal strife would eventually lead to the collapse of the Twentieth Dynasty.[114]

Image 200
-Pharaoh Ramses III-

Museum of Fine Arts,
Boston

Image 201
-Pharaoh Ramses III-

KhonsuTemple
Karnak, Egypt

PHARAOH RAMSES IV

Son of Pharaoh Ramses III

Name: King Ramses IV, 3rd   Pharaoh of The 20th Dynasty

Meaning Of Name: Ramses means "Ra bore him"

Aka: Ramesses

Born: Egypt, Africa

Years ruled: Approximately 31 years

Some Accomplishments: He became crown prince at the age of 12.[115]   Pharaoh Ramesses IV came to the throne under   difficult circumstances. His father, Pharaoh Ramesses III, was assassinated by conspirators led by Tiye (one of his secondary wives) to establish her own son Pentawer, Ramesses IV's half-brother, on the throne. Ramesses IV, however, was able to secure himself on the throne, and had the conspirators arrested and executed.[116]

Image 202
-Pharaoh Ramses IV-

British Museum
London

PHARAOH PIYE

Son of Pharaoh Kashta

Name: King Piye, 1ˢᵗ Pharaoh and founder of The 25ᵗʰ Dynasty

Meaning Of Name:

Aka: Pankhy or Piankhi

Born: Egypt, Africa

Years ruled: Approximately 30 years

Some Accomplishments: During Pharaoh Piye's reign, there was a period of rivalry and religious division amongst the rulers of lower, (northern), Egypt. To Piye, this presented an opportunity for both territorial expansion and religious revival.

As such, Pharaoh Piye initiated what he considered a Holy War in the name of Amun Ra, with the objective of uniting Upper and Lower Egypt under the Worship of Amun, (one of the Founding Gods of ancient Egypt).[117]

Pharaoh Piye expanded his power beyond Thebes into northern Egypt. As a result of this, Tefnakht of Sais formed a coalition between local kings of the Delta Region and had Piye's ally king Nimlot of Hermopolis defect to his side. Tefnakht then sent his coalition army south and besieged Herakleopolis where its king Peftjauawybast and the local commanders appealed to Pharaoh Piye for help.

Pharaoh Piye responded immediately. He marched north with his army and achieved complete victory at Herakleopolis. He conquered the cities of Hermopolis and Memphis among others and received the submission of the kings of the Nile Delta including Input II of

Leontopolis, Osorkon IV of Tanis and his former ally, Nimlot of Hermopolis. Tefnakht took refuge on an island in the Delta and formally conceded defeat in a letter to Pharaoh Piye.

Satisfied with his triumph, Pharaoh Piye sailed south to Thebes, Waset, and then to Nubia.[118]

After defeating the foreigners, and united upper, (southern), and lower, (northern), Egypt, Pharaoh Piye returned Egypt to its ancient cultural ways including the worship of the ancient Egyptian god, Amun.

The 25th Dynasty's reunification of Lower Egypt, Upper Egypt, and Kush created the largest Egyptian empire since the New Kingdom. They restored ancient Egyptian religious traditions, temples, and artistic forms. No images of Pharaoh Piye were located.

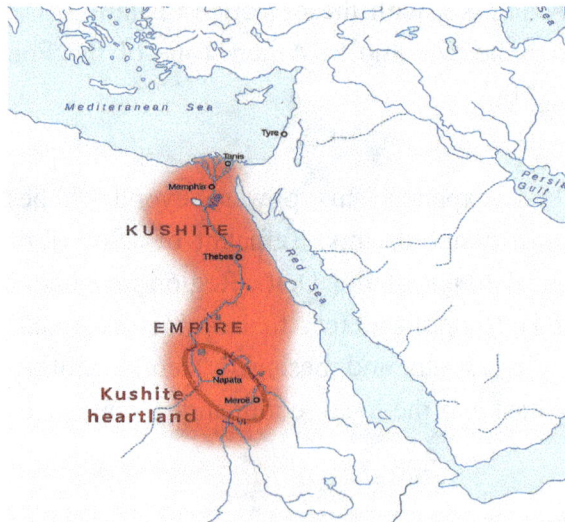

Image 203
-Egyptian Empire During
The 25th Dynasty-

PHARAOH SHABAKA

Son of Pharaoh Kashta

Name: King Shabaka, 2nd   Pharaoh of The 25th Dynasty

Meaning Of Name:

Aka: Shabako

Born: Egypt, Africa

Years ruled: Approximately 15 years

Some Accomplishments: Early in his reign, Pharaoh Shabako moved north, captured Boccoris and and kicked the foreigners out of Egypt. He returned Egypt to its ancient cultural ways including the worship of the ancient Egyptian god Amun.

The remainder of Shabako's reign seems to have been peaceful. He established his capital at Thebes, Waset, and fostered the priesthood and religious architecture. He restored the ancient temple at Thebes and completed much repair work on temples throughout Upper and Lower Egypt. He had old texts recopied and also continued the royal tradition of pyramid burials.   According to Herodotus, Pharaoh Shabako also abolished capital punishment in Egypt.[119]

Image 204
-Pharaoh Shabaqa-

Egyptian Museum
Cairo, Egypt

Image 205
-Pharaoh Shabaqa-

The British Museum
London

131

PHARAOH SHEBITKU

Son of Pharaoh Kashta

Name: King Shebitku, 3rd   Pharaoh of The 25th Dynasty

Meaning Of Name:

Aka: Shabataka or Shebitqo. He was called Sethos by the Greeks

Born: Egypt, Africa

Years ruled: Approximately 9 years

Some Accomplishments: He was the nephew and successor of Pharaoh Shabako. During his uncle's reign, there was a policy of conciliation and cooperation with the Assyrians. This kept the Assyrians from coming further into Egypt. Pharaoh Shebitku had a different policy, resistance.

A stela from Kawa tells of Shebitku asking his brothers, including Taharqa, to come to him at Thebes, Waset, from Nubia. The army went with Taharqa. On another stela, there is a story told that when Jerusalem was under attack by the Assyrians, that the king of Ethiopia (Kush) came against Sennacherib (of Assyria) to help Jerusalem. Shebitku joined in the resistance against Sennacherib and an Egyptian army was sent to Palestine, led by Shebitku's brother Taharqa.[120]

Image 206
-Pharaoh Shebitku -

Nubian Museum
Aswan, Egypt

132

PHARAOH TAHARQA
Son of Pharaoh Piye

Name: King Taharqa, 4th   Pharaoh of The 25th Dynasty

Meaning Of Name:

Aka: Tiharka, Taharka

Born: Egypt, Africa

Years ruled: Approximately 26 years

Some Accomplishments: Early in his reign Pharaoh Taharqa supported   Palestine's   resistance   against   King Sennacherib of Assyria.   Taharqa's   army   was   defeated   by   Sennacherib's   son Esarhaddon who captured Memphis.   The Assyrians set up a new Assyrian administration, entrusting the government and collection of tribute to the native chiefs. On Esarhaddon's withdrawal from Egypt, Taharqa returned from his refuge in upper, (southern), Egypt and massacred the Assyrian garrisons. He held control over Egypt until he was completely routed by Esarhaddon's son Ashurbanipal, after which he fled south to Nubia.[121]

Mainstream scholars agree that this is the same King Taharqa spoken of in the Bible.[122]

> 2 Kings 19:9, "And when he heard say of Tirhakah king of Ethiopia, Behold, he is come out to fight against thee:....".

> Isaiah 37:9, "And he heard say concerning Tirhakah king of Ethiopia, He is come forth to make war with thee. And when he heard it, he sent messengers to Hezekiah, saying...".

Image 207
-Pharaoh Taharqa-

The British Museum
London

Image 208
-Pharaoh Taharqa-

Ny Carlsberg Glyptotek
Copenhagen

Image 209
-Pharaoh Taharqa-

Louvre Museum
France

Image 210
-Pharaoh Taharqa-

PHARAOH TANTAMANI

Son of Pharaoh Shabaka

Name: King Tantamani, Last Pharaoh of The 25th Dynasty

Meaning Of Name:

Aka:

Born: Egypt, Africa

Years ruled: Unsure

Some Accomplishments: After the Assyrians gained control of lower, (northern), Egypt from his uncle, Pharaoh Taharqa, Necho I was appointed king. Pharaoh Tantamani invaded lower, (northern), Egypt in the hopes of restoring his family to the throne. Tantamani marched down the Nile and reoccupied lower, (northern), Egypt. Necho I, the Assyrians' representative, was killed in Tantamani's campaign.

The Assyrians led by Ashurbanipal returned to Egypt in force. Together with Psamtik I's army, which included Carian mercenaries, they fought a pitched battle in north Memphis (close to the temple of Isis) between the Serapeum and Abusir. Pharaoh Tantamani was defeated and fled to Upper, (southern), Egypt.[123]

Pharaoh Tantamani was the last native born African to rule a united Egypt.

Egypt has since been ruled by the Assyrians, the Persians, the Romans and the modern day lighter skinned Egyptians we see in Egypt today.

Again, the lighter skinned Egyptians we see today are not representative of the ancient Egyptians. They are a mix of the native born Africans and those that invaded and or migrated to Egypt over thousands of years.

Image 211
-Pharaoh Tantamani-

Kerma Museum
Sudan

Image 212
-Pharaoh Tantamani-

Kerma Museum
Sudan

Image 213
-Pharaoh Tantamani-

Portrait of Tantamani in
his tomb in El-Kurru

Image 214
-Pharaoh Tantamani-

Kerma Museum
Sudan

SOME GODS & GODDESSES OF ANCIENT EGYPT

Image 215
-God Amun-

Luxor Museum
Egypt

Image 216
-God Amun-

Metropolitan Museum
Of Art
New York

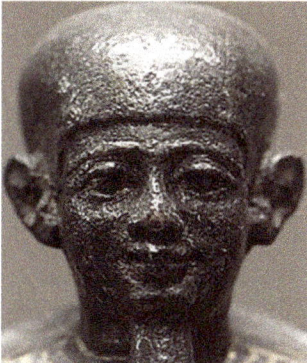

Image 217
-God Ptah-

Museum Of Art & History
Geneva, Switzerland

Image 218
-God Ptah-

Metropolitan Museum
Of Art
New York

Image 219
-Goddess Hathor-

Metropolitan Museum
Of Art
New York

Image 220
-Goddess Hathor-

Museum Carnuntinum
Austria

Image 221
-Goddess Isis-

Metropolitan Museum
Of Art

Image 222
-Goddess Isis-

Metropolitan Museum
Of Art

Image 223
-God Hapy-

The British Museum
London

Image 224
-God Hapy-

Petrie Museum of
Egyptian Archaeology
London

Image 225
-God Khonsu-

Cairo Museum
Egypt

Image 226
-God Khonsu-

Cairo Museum
Egypt

Image 227
-God Osiris-

Louvre Museum
France

Image 228
-God Osiris-

Location Unknown

Before I Close

Regardless of the observable tangible facts that have been presented in this book, which clearly prove the ancient Egyptians were black and brown Africans, some black ancient egyptian deniers will still discount these facts.

DNA studies

Some people trying to falsely prove a European connection to ancient Egypt will attempt to tell you that a recent DNA study conducted by the Max Planck Institute, in Germany, proves that the ancient Egyptians were more European than African.

What they will not tell you, is that only three (3) mummies were actually tested during this study. The oldest mummy tested was from the New Kingdom, 1,388 BC. Egypt at this point had already experienced two intermediate periods and was already thousands of years old. They will also not say that the youngest mummy tested was from 426 CE when Egypt was under Roman rule. Again, thousands of years after the founding of ancient Egypt and the Egyptian Dynasties by the indigenous African people.

To be clear, Egypt was united under Pharaoh Narmer approximately 3,000 BC. The oldest mummy tested was from 1,388 BC. The youngest mummy was from 426 CE. Simple math...

In addition, the three (3) mummies tested were all from a single site which, basically, logically, should cancel out any conclusion that ALL of the ancient Egyptians have European DNA. But, don't take my word for it, take the words of the researchers themselves who did the actual research:

"The oldest mummy sequenced was from the New Kingdom, 1,388 BCE, when Egypt was at the height of its power and glory. The youngest was from 426 CE, when the country was ruled from Rome. The ability to acquire genomic data on ancient Egyptians is a dramatic achievement, which opens up new avenues of research".

"One limitation according to their report, 'all our genetic data were obtained from a single site in Middle Egypt and may not be representative for all of ancient Egypt.' In southern Egypt they say, the genetic makeup of the people may have been different, being closer to the interior of the continent".

"Researchers in the future may want to determine exactly when sub-Saharan African genes seeped into the Egyptian genome and why. They'll also want to know where ancient Egyptians themselves came from. To do so, they'll have to identify older DNA from, as Krause said, 'Back further in time, in prehistory.'"[124]

So again, after this "conclusive" DNA sequencing, the unsubstantiated theory that no one knows where the ancient Egyptians came from is still promoted.

But wait, did you catch the racism embedded in the article or did they slip one past the goalie?

The article says, "Researchers in the future may want to determine exactly when sub-Saharan African genes seeped into the Egyptian genome and why..." Understand the misdirection that is taking place here. By sub-saharan they mean black people; insinuating that the ancient Egyptians were anything other than black and that at some point the "sub-Saharan" (black) African genes "seeped" into the Egyptian genome.

So, as we can cleary see, even in "scientific" research materials, the lie and inherent racism is still perpetuated.

A side note, it is genetically impossible to get black people from white people. But, it is genetically possible to get white people from black people. According to a Washington Post article, a large number of self proclaimed white, European, people are finding out through DNA testing that they are actually part African.[125]

In 1903, workmen digging a drainage trench in Gough's Cave in the Cheddar Gorge, in Somerset, England uncovered the remains of a young man, sealed under a stalagmite. The man was given the name "Cheddar Man".

Cheddar man is still the oldest virtually complete skeleton that has been unearthed in the British Isles. The study of the 10,000-year-old man surprised people when it revealed his blue eyes and dark skin.

Dr. Tom Booth, is a postdoctoral researcher working with the Natural History Museum in London. He has stated that, "...cheddar man has the genetic markers and skin pigmentation usually associated with sub-saharan ("black") Africa. This discovery is consistent with a number of other mesolithic human remains discovered throughout Europe". [126]

If you have not seen the reconstructed images of cheddar man, I highly suggest that you do so...[127,128]

Also research and/or google, "scientists reveal face of the first European".[129, 130]

Have a look. You may be surprised.

The red haired mummies

Another theory presented to support the false claim that the ancient Egyptians were Europeans are the red haired mummies. This is because some of the mummies from ancient Egypt appear to have red hair. Some use this as proof that the mummies were white people.

First, there are a number of black people that are born with natural red hair. More importantly, however, is the fact that only 1% to 2% of the worlds population have red hair,[131] this makes it highly unlikely that so many ancient Egyptians would have red hair. The more logical conclusion is that the red hair was a result of the mummification process.

Human hair contains a mixture of black-brown-yellow eumelanin and red pheomelanin. The black-brown-yellow eumelanin is less chemically stable than the red pheomelanin and breaks down faster when oxidized. It is for this reason that Egyptian mummies have reddish hair.[132]

In spite of the frequent claims of "scientific evidence" presented to "claim" a white ancient Egypt, or the vast number of Europeans portraying ancient Egyptians in movies or the mainstream Egyptologists claiming a non "sub saharan" influence on ancient Egypt, the reality is that the sculptures carvings and paintings left behind by the ancient Egyptians clearly shows the ancient Egyptians as they saw themselves – proud black and brown people from Africa.

Some people may experience cognitive dissonance with the evidence presented in this book. Others may accept the facts and adjust their beliefs.

Frantz Fanon, a psychiatrist and philosopher, describes cognitive dissonance as, "Sometimes people hold a core belief that is very strong. When they are presented with evidence that works against that belief, the new evidence cannot be accepted. It would create a feeling that is extremely uncomfortable, called cognitive dissonance. And because it is so important to protect the core belief, they will rationalize, ignore and even deny anything that doesn't fit in with the core belief".

He went on to further say that, "when presented with contradictory evidence, people may not change their erroneous belief but will strengthen it. Essentially, when your deepest convictions are challenged by accepted evidence, your beliefs will get stronger. The more evidence you give, the greater the resolve against it. Cognitive dissonance is about protecting a core assumption about how we perceive the world, so contradictory evidence is an assault on our familiar worldview."

Carl Richard Lepsius is considered to be the founder of modern Egyptology in Germany. During his excavations in Egypt, he made discoveries that changed his belief about the true identity of the ancient Egyptians. In his book "Denkmaler Aus Aegypten Und

Aethiopien Erganzungsband he wrote,"Where we expected to see an Egyptian, we saw an authentic negro". Again, differentiating between the modern day fair skin Egyptians and the "authentic" negro.

So, I ask, if you saw the people in this book walking down the street today, would you consider them to be black, a person of color or white..?

Conclusion

We believe we have succesfully exhibited factual, verifiable evidence and proof that the ancient Egyptians were black Africans and represented themselves as such. They left us their strong beautiful African faces, representing themselves and their Gods carved in stone.

Unfortunately, as a result of racism, we have been conditioned to believe that the ancient Egyptians were anything other than black people.

If you have reached the conclusion of this presentation and still believe the ancient Egyptians were anything other black Africans, I guess I should quote the words of George Costanza who said, "A lie is not a lie, if you believe it".

In reality, however, It may be necessary to step outside the conditioning and racist boundaries we have been subjected to in order to appreciate the real world and the people who live in it. As a society, we have to take the truth as authority and not authority as the truth.

Thank you for joining me on this journey. I hope you have found value in this presentation. This is not just a history book, It is a legacy book.

Always remember, He that knows not, and knows not, that he knows not, is asleep. Awaken him.

More to come...

Suggested Websites To Support

1. Sankofa Pan African Series on Youtube – Hosted by Bunmi Oyinsan
2. GoBlack2Africa on Youtube -
3. Earn Your Leisure on Youtube
4. Thehumanchessgame.com
5. Home Team History on Youtube

Suggested Reading Materials

FRESHMAN/WOMAN

1. From The Browder File 1 & 2 by Anthony Browder
2. Introduction To African Civilizations by Willis Nathaniel Huggins
3. Ancient Egypt Light Of The World by Gerald Massey
4. The Psychopathic Racial Personality by Bobby Wright
5. Nile Valley Contributions To Civilization by Anthony Browder
6. The Name Negro-Its Origin and Evil Use by Richard M. Moore
7. Breaking The Chains and Images of Pyshological Slavery by Na'im Akbar
8. The Condition, Elevation, Emigration and Destiny of the Colored People by Martin R. Delany
9. African Psychology by Wade Nobles
10. Essays In Ancient Egyptian Studies Science And Oppression by Jacob Carruthers

SOPHOMORE

1. African Glory: The Story of Vanished Negro Civilizations By J. C. Degraft Johnson
2. Destruction of Black Civilization by Dr. Chancellor Wiliams
3. The Mis-Education of the Negro by Carter G. Woodson
4. Africentricity by Molefi Asante
5. Nation Building by Kwame Agyei Akoto
6. New Dimensions in African History by Dr. John H. Clarke
7. The Choice: The Issue Of Black Survival In America by Samuel F. Yette
8. The Husia by Dr. Maulana Karenga

148

9. Origin of Race and Color by Edward Wilmont Blyden

10. The Oldest Book in the World (The Teachings of Ptah-Hotep) by Asa G. Hilliard

11. Wonderful Ethiopians of the Cushite Empire by Drusilla Dunjee Houston

12. Introduction to African Civilization by John G. Jackson

13. Kindezi: The Congo Art of Babysitting by K. Kia Bunseki Fu-Kiau

14. Christianity, Islam and The Negro Race by Edward Wilmot Blyden

15. Self Healing Power and Therapy by Kimbwandènde Kia Bunseki Fu-Kiau

16. J.A. Rogers: EVERYTHING

17. Dr. Ben: EVERYTHING

18. Dr. John H. Clark: EVERYTHING

JUNIOR

1. The Isis Papers by Dr. Francis Cress Welsing

2. The Rebirth of African Civilization by Dr. Chancellor Wiliams

3. Blueprint for Black Power by Dr. Amos Wilson

4. The Star of The Deep Beginnings by Dr. Charles Finch

5. Ancient Egypt & Black Africa by Dr. Theophile Obenga

6. Let The Ancestors Speak by Ankh Mi Ra

7. To Heal a People Edited by Erriel Kofi Addae

8. Intellectual Warfare by Dr. Jacob Carruthers

9. Echos of The Darkland by Charles Finch

10. Two Thousand Seasons by Ayi Kwei Armah

11. The Healers by Ayi Kwei Armah

12. Return to the Mother Principle by Dr. Oba T'Shaka

13. Ivan Van Sertima: Everything

14. Cheikh Anta Diop: Everything.

SENIOR

1. Civilization or Barbarism by Chiekh Anta Diop
2. Yurugu by Dr. Marimba Ani
3. Stolen Legacy by George James
4. African Philosophy: The Pharaonic Period: 2780 - 330 BC by Dr. Theophile Obenga
5. Pedagogy of the Oppressed by Paulo Freire
6. How Europe Underdeveloped Africa by Walter Rodney
7. Man God and Civilization by John G. Jackson

Bibliography

1. Egypte, Ancienne, 1939. J.J. Champollion-Figeac, 1839, pgs. 26-27
2. Voyages en Syrie Egypte, Paris, 1787, M.C.F. Volney I, pgs. 74-77.
3. https://dailynewsegypt.com/2007/09/27/tutankhamun-was-not-black-says-hawass/
4. https://dailynewsegypt.com/2021/04/14/claims-that-ancient-egyptians-were-african-untrue-zahi-hawass
5. https://dailynewsegypt.com/2007/09/27/tutankhamun-was-not-black-says-hawass/
6. Herodotus, Book II, p. 57
7. Aeschylus, the Suppliants, *vv* 719-720
8. Apollodorus, book II, The family of the Inachus', paras 3-4
9. Diogenes Lacrtius Book VII, 1.
10. Volney (M.C.F. Volney, Voyages en Syrie Egypte, Paris, 1787, Vol 1. pps 74-77
11. Ammianus Marcellinus, Book XXII, para 16 (23)
12. Aristotle, Physiognomy, p 6.
13. Diodorus (Universal History, Book III, The Antiquity Of The Ethiopian
14. http://africanknowledge.weebly.com/the-egyptians.html
15. https://www.smithsonianmag.com/travel/sudan-land-kush-meroe-ancient-civilization-overlooked-180975498/
16. https ://en.wikipedia.org/wiki/Medjay
17. Gardiner, Alan H. (1947). *Ancient Egyptian Onomastica*. Vol. 1. Oxford University Presg Gardiner (1947), pp. 82-85.
18. https://en.wikipedia.org/wiki/Narmer
19. https://www.britannica.com/biography/Menes
20. https://www.worldhistory.org/Narmer_Palette/
21. https://www.britannica.com/biography/Menes
22. https://egyptianmuseum.org/deities-ptah
23. https://www.livius.org/articles/person/den/
24. *https://en.wikipedia.org/wiki/Den (pharaoh)*
25. https://ancientegyptonline.co.uk/den/
26. http://www.touregypt.net/featurestories/ninetjer.htm
27. https://ancientegyptonline.co.uk/nynetjer/
28. *https://en.wikipedia.org/wiki/Khasekhemwy*
29. https ://www.britannica.com/biography/Khasekhemwy
30. https://www.britannica.com/biography/Djoser
31. https://egyptianmuseum.org/explore/old-kingdom-ruler-djoser
32. https://en.wikipedia.org/wiki/Imhotep
33. https://ancientegyptonline.co.uk/huni/
34. https://en.wikipedia.org/wiki/Sneferu
35. The Complete Royal Families of Ancient Egypt. Ed. Aidan Dodson & Dylan Hilton. Thames and Hudson Ltd: London, 2004.p. 50

36. https://en.wikipedia.org/wiki/Khufu
37. https://www.britannica.com/topic/Pyramids-of-Giza
38. https://www.discovery.com/exploration/Eight-Faces-Great-Pyramid-Giza#

39. https://en.wikipedia.org/wiki/Khufu Ship

40. https://en.wikipedia.org/wiki/Djedefre

41. https://ancientegyptonline.co.uk/djedefre/

42. https://en.wikipedia.org/wiki/Pyramid_of_Djedefre

43. https://ancientegyptonline.co.uk/khafre/
44. https://en.wikipedia.org/wiki/Menkaure_
45. https://www.britannica.com/biography/Menkaure-king-of-Egypt
46. https://www.britannica.com/biography/Menkaure-king-of-Egypt
47. https://en.wikipedia.org/wiki/Shepseskaf
48. Callender, Gae (2003) [2000]. "The Middle Kingdom Renaissance (c.2055–1650 BC)". In Shaw, Ian (ed.). *The Oxford History of Ancient Egypt*. Oxford, New York: Oxford University Press. ISBN 9780191604621 p. 140-141.
49. Vandersleyen, Claude (1994). "La titulature de Montouhotep II". In Bryan, Betsy Morrell; Lorton, David (eds.)
50. Essays in Egyptology in honor of Hans Goedicke (in Italian). San Antonio, Texas: Van Siclen Books. pp. 317–320. ISBN 09331754 0X. OCLC 34552368.
51. http://www.touregypt.net/featurestories/mentuhotep2.htm
52. https://en.wikipedia.org/wiki/Mentuhotep_III
53. http://www.touregypt.net/featurestories/amenemhet1
54. https://ancientegyptonline.co.uk/senusreti/
55. https://www.britannica.com/biography/Sesostris-I
56. Grajetzki, The Middle Kingdom of Ancient Egypt: History, p. 38–41
57. https://www.britannica.com/biography/Sesostris-I
58. Peter Clayton, Chronicle of the Pharaohs, Thames & Hudson Ltd, (1994), p.78
59. https://www.britannica.com/biography/Amenemhet-II
60. Callender, Gae (2004). "The Middle Kingdom Renaissance (c.2055–1650 BC)". In Shaw, Ian (ed.)The Oxford History of Ancient Egypt.. Oxford: Oxford University Press. Pgs. 137-171p. ISBN 978-0-19-815034-3. p. 152.
61. https://en.wikipedia.org/wiki/Senusret_II
62. Clayton, Peter (1994).Chronicle of the Pharaohs, London: Thames & Hudson Ltd. ISBN 978-0-500-050474-3. p 137-138.
63. Herodotus, Book II, p. 104
64. "The Pyramids: Their Archeology and History", Miroslav Verner, Translated by Steven Rendall,p386-387 & p416-421, Atlantic, ISBN 1-84354-171-8.

65. https://www.britannica.com/biography/Sesostris-III
66. https://www.worldhistory.org/Senusret_III/
67. https://en.wikipedia.org/wiki/Amenemhat_III
68. https://www.britannica.com/biography/Amenemhet-III
69. https://en.wikipedia.org/wiki/Amenemhat_IV
70. http://www.touregypt.net/12dyn07.htm _
71. https://www.britannica.com/biography/Sebeknefru
72. https://www.journals.uchicago.edu/doi/abs/10.1086/716826? journalCode=nea
73. Grimal, Nicolas (1988).*A History of Ancient Egypt*. Librairie Arthéme Fayard.p. 192
74. https://en.wikipedia.org/wiki/Ahmose_I
75. Maspero, Gaston. History of Egypt, Chaldean, Syria, Babylonia and Assyria, Volume *4 (of 12),* Project Gutenberg EBook, Release Date: December 16, 2005. EBook #17324
76. https://www.theguardian.com/science/2021/dec/28/egyptian-pharaohs-mummified-body-gives-up-its-secrets-after-3500-years
77. https://www.britannica.com/biography/Thutmose-I
78. Shaw, Ian & Nicholson, Paul (1995). The Dictionary of Ancient Egypt. The British Museum Press. p. 289.
79. https://www.ancient-egypt-online.com/thutmose-II.html

80. https://en.wikipedia.org/wiki/Hatshepsut

81. Ancient Egyptian Literature. Univ of California Press. p. 340. ISBN 9780520305847
82. https://en.wikipedia.org/wiki/Thutmose_III#cite_note-16
83. Strudwick, Helen (2006). *The Encyclopedia of Ancient Egypt*. New York: Sterling Publishing Co., Inc. pp. 72–73 ISBN 978-1-4351-4654-9.
84. J.H. Breasted, Ancient Times: A History of the Early World; An Introduction to the Study of Ancient History and the Career of Early Man. Outlines of European History 1. Boston: Ginn and Company, 1914, p.85.
85. https://www.britannica.com/biography/Thutmose-III

86. https://en.wikipedia.org/wiki/Amenhotep_II
87. https://www.britannica.com/biography/Pharaoh-Thutmose-IV
88. https://www.britannica.com/biography/Pharaoh-Thutmose-IV
89. https://en.wikipedia.org/wiki/Thutmose_IV
90. https://en.wikipedia.org/wiki/Amenhotep_III
91. https://www.britannica.com/biography/Amenhotep-III
92. https://en.wikipedia.org/wiki/Akhenaten
93. https://www.britannica.com/biography/Akhenaten
94. Zaki, Mey (2008). The Legacy of Tutankhamun: Art and History. Photographs by Farid Atiya. Giza, Egypt: Farid Atiya Press. ISBN 978-977-17-4930-1, https://wikikipedia.org/wiki/Akhenaten_

95. https://www.britannica.com/biography/Tutankhamun
96. https://www.britannica.com/biography/Ay-king-of-Egypt.

97. https://en.wikipedia.org/wiki/Horemheb
98. https://www.worldhistory.org/Horemheb/
99. https://www.britannica.com/biography/Ramses-I
100.   https://en.wikipedia.org/wiki/Seti_I
101.   https://www.britannica.com/biography/Seti-I
102.   https://en.wikipedia.org/wiki/Ramesses_II
103.   https://historyguild.org/the-battle-of-kadesh-and-the-worlds-first-peace-treaty/

104.   https://www.britannica.com/biography/Ramses-II- king-of-Egypt/Prosperity-during-the-reign-of- Ramses-II

105.   https://en.wikipedia.org/wiki/Merneptah
106.   Peter Clayton, Chronicle of the Pharaohs, Thames & Hudson Ltd, 1994. p.158
107.   https://en.wikipedia.org/wiki/Seti_II

108.   https://en.wikipedia.org/wiki/Seti_II

109.   https://pharaoh.se/pharaoh/Amenmesse

110.   http://www.touregypt.net/featurestories/siptah.htm
111.   https://ancientegyptonline.co.uk/tausret/
112.   https://en.wikipedia.org/wiki/Setnakhte
113.   Barbara Cifola (1988), Ramses III and the Sea   Peoples: A Structural Analysis of the Medinet Habu   Inscriptions, NOVA SERIES, Vol. 57, No. 3 (1988),   pp. 275-306.
114.   https://en.wikipedia.org/wiki/Ramesses_III
115.   .A. J. Peden, The Reign of Ramesses IV, Aris &   Phillips Ltd, 1994, Jacobus Van Dijk, 'The Amarna   Period and the later New Kingdom' in The Oxford   History of Ancient Egypt, ed. Ian Shaw, Oxford University Press paperback, 2002, p.306
116.   https://en.wikipedia.org/wiki/Ramesses_IV
117.   https://www.afrikaiswoke.com/king-piye-ancient- nubias-greatest/
118.   https://en.wikipedia.org/wiki/Piye
119.   https://biography.yourdictionary.com/shabaka
120.   http://www.touregypt.net/25dyn02.htm
121.   https://www.britannica.com/biography/Taharqa
122.   Aubin, Henry T. (2002). The Rescue of Jerusalem. New York, NY: Soho Press, Inc. pp. X, 127, 129–130, 139–152. ISBN 1-56947-275-0.
154

123.	https://en.wikipedia.org/wiki/Tantamani

124.	https://bigthink.com/surprising-science/were-the-ancient-egyptians-black-or-white-scientists-now-know/

125.	https://www.washingtonpost.com/local/social-issues/they-considered-themselves-white-but-dna-tests-told-a-more-complex-story/2018/02/06/16215d1a-e181-11e7-8679-a9728984779c_story.html

126.	https://www.nhm.ac.uk/discover/cheddar-man-mesolithic-britain-blue-eyed-boy.html

127.	http://www.sci-news.com/othersciences/anthropology/cheddar-mans-face-05745.html

128.	https://www.nhm.ac.uk/discover/cheddar-man-mesolithic-britain-blue-eyed-boy.html

129.	https://www.dailymail.co.uk/sciencetech/article-1177123/The-European-Created-fragments-fossil-face-forbears-35-000-years-ago.html

130.	https://www.telegraph.co.uk/news/worldnews/europe/romania/5273654/Scientists-reveal-face-of-the-first-European.html

131.	https://www.bbc.com/news/magazine-24331615#:~:text=It%20is%20often%20said%20that,the%20size%20of%20its%20population.

132.	http://www.chm.bris.ac.uk/motm/melanin/melaninh.htm

Images

1. Map Of Africa courtesy of -
   <ahref="https://www.freepik.com/vectors/travel">Travel vector created by freepik – www.freepik.com</a>
2. Pharaoh Narmer – Courtesy of Wikipedia.com - This image is in the "Public Domain"
3. Pharaoh Sahure – Courtesy of - Museum Of Art, New York - This image is in the "Public Domain"
4. Pharaoh Mentuhotep II – Courtesy of – https://commons.wikimedia.org/wiki/File:Montouhotep_II - This file is licensed under the Creative Commons Attribution-Share Alike 4.0 International license.
5. Pharaoh Amenhotep III Courtesy of – https://commons.wikimedia.org/wiki/File:Portrait_head_of_pharaoh_Amenhotep_III_with_nemes_and_double_crown_01.jpg - This file is licensed under the Creative Commons Attribution-Share Alike 4.0 International license.
6. Pharaoh Akhenaten – Courtesy of – https://www.flickr.com/photos/leswilliamsphotography/15462699390 - This file is licensed under the Creative Commons Attribution-Share Alike 2.0 Generic (CC BY-SA 2.0.
7. Pharaoh Tiharka – Courtesy of https://commons.wikimedia.org/wiki/File:Taharqa,_ca._690-64_BCE,_Ny_Carlsberg_Glyptotek,_Copenhagen_(36420740125).jpg - This file is licensed under the Creative Commons Attribution-Share Alike 2.0 Generic
8. Pharaoh Senusret III - Courtesy of – https://commons.wikimedia.org/wiki/File:Sesostris_III_Sphinxkopf.jpg -This file is licensed under the Creative Commons Attribution-Share Alike 3.0 Unported, 2.5 Generic, 2.0 Generic and 1.0 Generic license
9. Egyptian Army – Courtesy of – https://commons.wikimedia.org/wiki/File:Soldats_de_l%27arm%C3%A9e_%C3%89gyptienne.jpg - This file is licensed under the Creative Commons Attribution-Share Alike 4.0 International license.
10. Egyptian Sailors – Courtesy of - https://en.wikipedia.org/wiki/Ancient_maritime_history – This image is in the "Public Domain".
11. Egyptian Sailors – Courtesy of - https://www.pikist.com/free-photo-vjcju - This image is in the "Public Domain".
12. Pharaoh Tutankhamun – Courtesy of - https://commons.wikimedia.org/wiki/File:Head_of_King_Tutankhamen-11.1533-IMG_4848-gradient.jpg - This file is licensed under the Creative Commons Attribution-ShareAlike 3.0 France license.

13. Princess of Pharaoh Akhenatens family – Courtesy of -
https://commons.wikimedia.org/wiki/File:Princess_of_Akhenaton_family
-E_14715-IMG_0319-gradient.jpg-This file is licensed under the Creative
Commons Attribution-Share Alike 3.0 France license.

14. Egyptian Craftsmen – Courtesy of
https://en.wikipedia.org/wiki/File:Egyptian_Farmers.jpg. - This file is
licensed under the Creative Commons Attribution-Share Alike 4.0
International license.

15. God Amun – Courtesy of -
https://commons.wikimedia.org/wiki/File:Head_of_the_god_Amun_MET
_DT11639.jpg - This image is in the "Public Domain".

16. Pharaoh Amenhotep III – Courtesy of -
https://es.wikipedia.org/wiki/Archivo:Cabeza_de_Amenhotep_III_(Britis
h_Museum).jpg - This file is licensed under the Creative Commons
Atribucion-CompartirIgual 4.0 Internacional.

17. Pharaoh Tutankhamun – Courtesy of -
https://commons.wikimedia.org/wiki/File:Tutanhkamun_tomb_statue_edit
_1.jpg - This image is in the "Public Domain".

18. God Ptah - Courtesy of -
https://commons.wikimedia.org/wiki/File:Head,_Ptah_MET_m2600_fron
t.jpg - This image is in the Public Domain.

19. Queen Nefertiti – Courtesy of
https://commons.wikimedia.org/wiki/File:Nuovo_regno,_xviii_dinastia,_r
egno_di_amenhotep_IV,_ritratto_di_nefertiti,_da_karnak_1353-
1347_ac_ca.jpg - This file is licensed under the Creative Commons
Attribution 3.0 Unported license.

20. Princess Meritamun – Courtesy of
https://commons.wikimedia.org/wiki/File:Akhmim6.jpg - This file is
licensed under This file is licensed under the Creative Commons
Attribution 3.0 Share Alike Unported license.

21. Queen Ahmose Nefertari – Courtesy of
https://en.wikipedia.org/wiki/Ahmose-Nefertari - This file is licensed
under This file is licensed under the Creative Commons Attribution 4.0
Share Alike International license.

22. Queen Tiye – Courtesy of -
https://commons.wikimedia.org/wiki/File:Queen_Tiy_N2312_E25493_m
p3h8763.jpg- This file is licensed under the Creative Commons
Attribution-Share Alike 2.0 France license.

23. Medu Neter – Courtesy of - https://www.needpix.com/photo/256019/ -
This file is made available under the Creative Commons CC0 1.0
Universal Public Domain Dedication.

24. Pharaoh Narmer - Courtesy of
https://commons.wikimedia.org/wiki/File:Limestone_head_of_a_king._T
hought_by_Petrie_to_be_Narmer._Bought_by_Petrie_in_Cairo,_Egypt._1
st_Dynasty._The_Petrie_Museum_of_Egyptian_Archaeology,_London.jp
g - This file is licensed under the Creative Commons Attribution 4.0
Share Alike International license

25. Pharaoh Narmer – Courtesy of - https://commons.wikimedia.org/wiki/File:Menes.jpg – This image is in the Public Domain

26. Narmer Palette Front Side - Courtesty of -https://commons.wikimedia.org/wiki/File:Narmer_Palette.jpg - This image is in the Public Domain

27. Narmer Palette Reverse Side - Courtesty of -https://commons.wikimedia.org/wiki/File:Narmer_Palette.jpg - This image is in the Public Domain

28. Pharaoh Den – Courtesy of - https://commons.wikimedia.org/wiki/File:IvoryLabelOfDen-BritishMuseum-August19-08.jpg - This file is licensed under the Creative Commons Attribution-Share Alike 3.0 Unported license.

29. Pharaoh Den – Courtesy of - https://commons.wikimedia.org/wiki/File:Den_label.jpg - This file is licensed under the Creative Commons Attribution 2.0 Generic license.

30. Pharaoh Nynejeter – Courtesy of - https://commons.wikimedia.org/wiki/File:Statue_of_Ninetjer_Rijksmuseum_van_Oudheden_02.jpg- This file is licensed under the Creative Commons Attribution 3.0 Unported license. This image was cropped.

31. Pharaoh Nynejeter – Courtesy of https://commons.wikimedia.org/wiki/File:Statue_of_Ninetjer_Rijksmuseum_van_Oudheden_03.jpg. - This file is licensed under the Creative Commons Attribution 3.0 Unported license. This image was cropped

32. Pharaoh Khasekhemwy - Courtesy of https://commons.wikimedia.org/wiki/File:Khasekhem_oxford2.jpg - This file is licensed under the Creative Commons Attribution 3.0 Unported license.

33. Pharaoh Khasekhemwy - Courtesy of https://en.wikipedia.org/wiki/File:Khasekhemwy_statue_Ashmolean.JPG - This file is licensed under the Creative Commons Attribution-Share Alike 4.0 International, 3.0 Unported, 2.5 Generic license - This image was cropped

34. Pharaoh Djoser – Courtesy of https://commons.wikimedia.org/wiki/File:Djoser_a.gif – This image is in the Public Domain - This image was cropped

35. Pharaoh Djoser – Courtesy of https://en.wikipedia.org/wiki/Djoser - This image is in the Public Domain - This image was cropped

36. Stepped Pyramid At Saqqara – Courtesy of https://commons.wikimedia.org/wiki/File:Flickr_-_calewoodley_-_Pyramid_of_Djoser,_Saqqara.jpg - This file is licensed under the Creative Commons Attribution 2.0 Generic license.

37. Stepped Pyramid at Saqqara recreated – Courtesy of https://commons.wikimedia.org/wiki/File:LSR_Pharao_-_Pyramide_Djoser.jpg - This file is licensed under the Creative Commons Attribution-Share Alike 4.0 International.

38. Imhotep – Courtesy of
https://www.metmuseum.org/art/collection/search/548300- This image is
in the Public Domain - This image was cropped

39. Imhotep – Courtesy of
https://www.flickr.com/photos/edenpictures/42918535500 - Attribution
2.0 Generic (CC BY 2.0)

40. Pharaoh Huni – Courtesy of
https://commons.wikimedia.org/wiki/File:Huni-
StatueHead_BrooklynMuseum.png - This file is licensed under the
Creative Commons Attribution-Share Alike 2.5 Generic license

41. Pharaoh Huni – Courtesy of https://en.wikipedia.org/wiki/Huni– This
image is in the Public Domain

42. Pharaoh Sneferu – Courtesy of
https://commons.wikimedia.org/wiki/File:Snefru_hed-seb_festival.jpg -
This file is licensed under the Creative Commons Attribution 2.0 Generice
license.

43. Pharaoh Sneferu's Meidum Pyramid – Courtesy of
https://en.wikipedia.org/wiki/Meidum- Attribution 2.0 Generic (CC BY
2.0)

44. Pharaoh Sneferu's Bent Pyramid – Courtesy of
https://commons.wikimedia.org/wiki/File:Snefru
%27s_Bent_Pyramid_in_Dahshur.jpg - This file is licensed under the
Creative Commons Attribution 3.0 Unported license.

45. Pharaoh Sneferu's Bent Pyramid – Courtesy of
https://sv.m.wikipedia.org/wiki/Fil:Snofru%27s-Red-Pyramid.jpg- This
file is licensed under the Creative Commons Attribution 3.0

46. Pharaoh Khufu – This image is in the Public Domain

47. Pharaoh Khufu – This image is in the Public Domain

48. Great Pyramid At Giza – Courtesy of
https://commons.wikimedia.org/wiki/File:Kheops-Pyramid.jpg - This file
is licensed under the Creative Commons Attribution 3.0 Unported license.

49. Great Pyramid At Giza Inner Structure – Courtesy of
https://en.wikipedia.org/wiki/File:Cheops-Pyramid.svg - This file is
licensed under th Creative Commons Attribution-Share Alike 4.0
International license.

50. The Three Pyramids At Giza – Courtesy of
https://commons.wikimedia.org/wiki/File:All_Gizah_Pyramids-3.jpg -
This file is licensed under th Creative Commons Attribution-Share Alike
2.0 Generic license.

51. The Khufu Ship – Courtesy of
https://commons.wikimedia.org/wiki/File:By_ovedc_-_Khufu_ship_-
_16.jpg - This file is licensed under th Creative Commons Attribution-
Share Alike 4.0 International license.

52. Ancient Egyptian Sailors – Courtesy of https://www.pikist.com/free-
photo-vjcju/fr - This file is licensed under the Creative Commons
Attribution-Share Alike 2.0 Generic license.

53. The Khufu Ship – Courtesy of
https://en.wikipedia.org/wiki/Khufu_ship#/media/File:Model_of_Khufu's
_solar_barque.jpg – This image is in the Public Domain

54. Ancient Egyptian Sailors – Courtesy of
https://www.wallpaperflare.com/egypt-cairo-museum-archaeology-boat-
funeral-votive-characters-wallpaper-gcqjd- This image is in the Public
Domain

55. Pharaoh Djedefre - Courtesy of
https://commons.wikimedia.org/wiki/File:Djedefre_sphinx_head-
E_12626-IMG_4294-black.jpg - This file is licensed under the Creative
Commons Attribution-Share Alike 3.0 France.

56. Pharaoh Djedefre - Courtesy of
https://commons.wikimedia.org/wiki/File:Djedefre-head.jpg – This image
is in the Public Domain.

57. Djedefre Pyramid Reconstruction – Courtesy of
https://commons.wikimedia.org/wiki/File:Dyedefra_3D-1.jpg - This file
is licensed under the Creative Commons Attribution-Share Alike 3.0
Unported license.

58. Djedefre Pyramid 3d Reconstruction – Courtesy of
https://commons.wikimedia.org/wiki/File:008_Djedefre1.jpg - This file is
licensed under the Creative Commons Attribution-Share Alike 3.0
Unported license.

59. Pharaoh Khafre – https://commons.wikimedia.org/wiki/File:Khephren
%2BHorus.jpg - This file is licensed under the Creative Commons
Attribution-Share Alike 4.0 internatioal license.

60. Pharaoh Khafre – Courtesy of
https://commons.wikimedia.org/wiki/File:Khafra.jpg - This file is licensed
under the Attribution 2.0 Generic license.

61. Great Sphinx At Giza – Courtesy of
https://commons.wikimedia.org/wiki/File:Khafre.jpg - This image is in
the Public Domain.

62. Pharaoh Menkaure – Courtesy of
https://commons.wikimedia.org/wiki/File:Khephren%2BHorus.jpg - This
file is licensed under the Attribution 4.0 International license.

63. Pharaoh Menkaure – Courtesy of
https://commons.wikimedia.org/wiki/File:Colossal_statue_of_Menkura-
09.204-IMG_4557.JPG- This file is licensed under the Creative
Commons Attribution-Share Alike 3.0 France license.

64. Menkaure Pyramid – Courtesy of
https://commons.wikimedia.org/wiki/File:The_Menkaure_Pyramid.jpg -
This file is licensed under the Creative Commons Attribution-Share Alike
3.0 Unported license.

65. Pharaoh Shepseskaf – Courtesy of
https://commons.wikimedia.org/wiki/File:Fragmentary_statue_head_of_
Menkaura_in_Boston.jpg - This file is licensed under the Creative
Commons Attribution-Share Alike 3.0 Unported license.

66. Pharaoh Mentuhotep II – Courtesy of https://www.metmuseum.org/art/collection/search/544008 – This image is in the Public Domain.

67. Pharaoh Mentuhotep II – Courtesy of https://commons.wikimedia.org/wiki/File:Montouhotep_II.jpg - This file is licensed under the Creative Commons Attribution-Share Alike 4.0 internatioal license.

68. Pharaoh Mentuhotep II – Courtesy of https://commons.wikimedia.org/wiki/File:Xi_dinastia,_rilievo_con_re_me ntoehotep_II,_da_tebe,_2009-1959_ac_ca.jpg - This file is licensed under the Creative Commons Attribution-Share Alike 3.0 Unported license.

69. Pharaoh Mentuhotep II – Courtesy of - https://commons.wikimedia.org/wiki/File:Mentuhotep-OsirideStatue-CloseUp_MuseumOfFineArtsBoston.png - This file is licensed under the Creative Commons Attribution-Share Alike 2.5 Generic license

70. Pharaoh Mentuhop II's Temple – Courtesy of https://commons.wikimedia.org/wiki/File:Mentuhotep-Tempel_01.JPG - This file is licensed under the Creative Commons Attribution-Share Alike 3.0 Unported license.

71. Pharaoh Mentuhop II's Temple Reconstructed Courtesy of - - https://commons.wikimedia.org/wiki/File:MentuhotepII-Tempel-Rekonstruktion.JPG – This image is in the Public Domain

72. Pharaoh Mentuhotep III – Courtesy of https://commons.wikimedia.org/wiki/File:Luxor_Museum_Statue_Mentu hotep_III._01.jpg - This file is licensed under the Creative Commons Attribution-Share Alike 3.0 Unported license.

73. Pharaoh Mentuhotep III – Courtesy of https://www.metmuseum.org/art/collection/search/545879 – This image is in the Public Domain

74. Pharaoh Amenemhat I – Courtesy of https://www.metmuseum.org/art/collection/search/544206 - This image is in the Public Domain

75. Pharaoh Amenemhat I – Courtesy of https://www.metmuseum.org/art/collection/search/545105- This image is in the Public Domain

76. Pharaoh Senusret I – Courtesy of https://commons.wikimedia.org/wiki/File:-1950_Sesostris_I_anagoria.JPG - This file is licensed under the Creative Commons Attribution-Share Alike 3.0 Unported license.

77. Pharaoh Senusret I – Courtesy of https://commons.wikimedia.org/wiki/File:Luxor_Museum_Statue_Sesostr is_I._01.jpg - This file is licensed under the Creative Commons Attribution-Share Alike 3.0 Unported license.

78. Pharaoh Senusret I – Courtesy of https://commons.wikimedia.org/wiki/File: %C3%84gyptisches_Museum_Leipzig_104.jpg - This file is licensed

under the Creative Commons Attribution-Share Alike 3.0, 2.5 Unported, 2.5 Generic, 2.0 Generic and 1.0 Generic license.

79. Pharaoh Senusret I – Courtesy of https://commons.wikimedia.org/wiki/File:I.Szenuszert.JPG - This file is licensed under the Creative Commons Attribution-Share Alike 2.5 Generic license

80. Pharaoh Amenemhat II – Courtesy of https://commons.wikimedia.org/wiki/File:Great_sphinx-A_23-IMG_8383-black.jpg - This file is licensed under the Creative Commons Attribution-Share Alike 3.0 France license.

81. Pharaoh Amenemhat II – Courtesy of https://commons.wikimedia.org/wiki/File:Great_Sphynx,_Louvre_2009.jpg - This file is licensed under the Creative Commons Attribution-Share Alike 2.0 Generic license.

82. Pharaoh Senusret II – Courtesy of https://commons.wikimedia.org/wiki/File:Upper_part_of_portrait_statue_of_pharaoh_Sesostris_II_with_nemes_and_ritual_beard_01.jpg - This file is licensed under the Creative Commons Attribution-Share Alike 4.0 international license.

83. Pharaoh Senusret II – Courtesy of https://commons.wikimedia.org/wiki/File:Statue_Senusret_II_Lille.jpg - This file is licensed under the Creative Commons Attribution-Share Alike 4.0 international license.

84. Pharaoh Senusret II – Courtesy of https://commons.wikimedia.org/wiki/File:Statue_Senusret_II_Petrie.jpg – This image is in the Public Domain

85. Pharaoh Senusret II – Courtesy of https://commons.wikimedia.org/wiki/File:Copenhagen_2018-01-14_(39149415244).jpg - This file is licensed under the Creative Commons Attribution-Share Alike 2.0 Generic license.

86. Procession Of The Aamu – Courtesy of https://commons.wikimedia.org/wiki/File:Procession_of_the_Aamu,_Tomb_of_Khnumhotep_II_(composite).jpg – This image is in the Public Domain

87. Procession Of The Aamu Recreated – Courtesy of https://commons.wikimedia.org/wiki/File:Drawing_of_the_procession_of_the_Aamu_group_tomb_of_Khnumhotep_II_at_Beni_Hassan.jpg - This file is licensed under the Creative Commons Attribution-Share Alike 3.0 Unported license.

88. Pharaoh Senusret III – Courtesy of https://cs.m.wikipedia.org/wiki/Soubor:StatueOfSesotrisIII-EA684-BritishMuseum-August19-08.jpg - This file is licensed under the Creative Commons Attribution-Share Alike 3.0 Unported license.

89. Pharaoh Senusret III – Courtesy of https://commons.wikimedia.org/wiki/File:Sen-useret_III,_Egypt,_Middle_Kingdom,_12th_Dynasty,_c._1874-1855_BCE_-_Nelson-Atkins_Museum_of_Art_-_DSC08148.JPG – This

image is in the Public Domain

90. Pharaoh Senusret III – Courtesy of
https://commons.wikimedia.org/wiki/File:Sesostris_III_Sphinxkopf.jpg -
This file is licensed under the Creative Commons Attribution-Share Alike
3.0 Unported, 2.5 Generic, 2.0 Generic license.

91. Pharaoh Senusret III – Courtesy of
https://commons.wikimedia.org/wiki/File:Senusret_III,_MET_Museum_
NYC.jpg - This file is licensed under the Creative Commons Attribution-
Share Alike 4.0 International license.

92. Pharaoh Amenemhat III - Courtesy of
https://commons.wikimedia.org/wiki/File:Amenemhat_III_in_panther_ski
n,_12th_dynasty.jpg - This file is licensed under the Creative Commons
Attribution-Share Alike 4.0 International license.

93. Pharaoh Amenemhat III - Courtesy of
https://commons.wikimedia.org/wiki/File:Amenemhat_III-N_464-
IMG_9947-white.jpg - This file is licensed under the Creative Commons
Attribution-Share Alike 3.0 France license.

94. Amenemhat IV – Courtesy of –
https://www.metmuseum.org/art/collection/search/544177 - this image is
in the Public Domain

95. Amenemhat IV – Courtesy of –
https://www.metmuseum.org/art/collection/search/544177 - this image is
in the Public Domain

96. Pharaoh Sobekneferu – Courtesy of
https://en.wikipedia.org/wiki/File:Statue_of_Sobekneferu_(Berlin_Egypti
an_Museum_14475).jpg – This image is in the Public Domain

97. Pharaoh Sobekneferu – Courtesy of
https://commons.wikimedia.org/wiki/File:Louvre_0320O7_01.jpg - This
image is in the Public Domain.

98. Pharaoh Ahmose I – Courtesy of
https://commons.wikimedia.org/wiki/File:Head_of_King_Amasis,_rewor
ked_for_a_non-royal_individual_MET_DP219656.jpg – This image is in
the Public Domain

99. Pharaoh Ahmose I – Courtesy of
https://www.metmuseum.org/art/collection/search/544885 – This image is
in the Public Domain.

100. Pharaoh Ahmose I – Courtesy of
https://commons.wikimedia.org/wiki/File:Iahmes-E_15682-IMG_0063-
gradient.jpg - This file is licensed under the Creative Commons
Attribution-Share Alike 3.0 France license.

101. Pharaoh Ahmose I – Courtesy of
https://commons.wikimedia.org/wiki/File:Head_of_King_Amasis,_rewor
ked_for_a_non-royal_individual_MET_DP219660.jpg - This image is in
the Public Domain

102. Pharaoh Amenhotep I – Courtesy of
https://commons.wikimedia.org/wiki/File:Nuovo_regno,_XVIII_dinastia,

_rilievo_frammentario_di_amenhotep_I,_1525-1504_ac_ca.jpg - This file is licensed under the Creative Commons Attribution-Share Alike 3.0 Unported license.

103. Pharaoh Amenhotep I – Courtesy of https://www.metmuseum.org/art/collection/search/587532 – This image is in the Public Domain

104. Pharaoh Thuthmise I – Courtesy of https://www.flickr.com/photos/prof_richard/48820159963/in/photostream/ - Attribution 2.0 Generic (CC BY 2.0)

105. Pharaoh Thuthmise I – Courtesy of https://commons.wikimedia.org/wiki/File:ColossalSandstoneHeadOfThutmoseI-BritishMuseum-August19-08.jpg - This file is licensed under the Creative Commons Attribution-Share Alike 3.0 Unported license.

106. Pharaoh Thuthmise I – Courtesy of https://www.flickr.com/photos/prof_richard/48820165458/in/photostream/ - Attribution 2.0 Generic (CC BY 2.0)

107. Pharaoh Thuthmise I – Courtesy of https://www.flickr.com/photos/prof_richard/48820514561/in/photostream/ - - Attribution 2.0 Generic (CC BY 2.0)

108. Wall Painting – Courtesy of - https://commons.wikimedia.org/wiki/File:Thutmose_I,_MET_Museum,_NYC.jpg - This file is licensed under the Creative Commons Attribution-Share Alike 4.0 international license.

109. Pharaoh Hatshephut - Courtesy of https://www.metmuseum.org/art/collection/search/549032 – This image is in the Public Domain

110. Pharaoh Hatshephut - Courtesy of https://commons.wikimedia.org/wiki/File:Osiride_head_of_Hatshepsut_2.jpg - This file is licensed under the Creative Commons Attribution-Share Alike 3.0 Unported license.

111. Pharaoh Hatshephut - Courtesy of https://www.metmuseum.org/art/collection/search/544448 - This image is in the Public Domain

112. Pharaoh Hatshephut - Courtesy of https://www.metmuseum.org/art/collection/search/544447 - This image is in the Public Domain

113. Pharaoh Hatshephut - Courtesy of https://commons.wikimedia.org/wiki/File:Head_and_Shoulders_of_a_Sphinx_of_Hatshepsut_MET_266796.jpg - This image is in the Public Domain

114. Pharaoh Hatshephut - Courtesy of https://commons.wikimedia.org/wiki/File:HatshepsutStatuette_MuseumOfFineArtsBoston.png - This file is licensed under the Creative Commons Attribution-Share Alike 2.5 Generic license.

115. Temple Of Hatshephut - Courtesy of https://commons.m.wikimedia.org/wiki/File:Temple_of_Hatshepsut_2,_D

eir_el-Bahari,_Luxor,_Egypt.jpg - Attribution: © Vyacheslav
Argenberg / http://www.vascoplanet.com/ - This file is licensed under the
Creative Commons Attribution-Share Alike 4.0 international license.

116.	Temple Of Hatshephut - Courtesy of
https://commons.m.wikimedia.org/wiki/File:Hatshepsut_Temple_R03.jpg
- This file is licensed under the Creative Commons Attribution-Share
Alike 4.0 international license.

117.	Temple Of Hatshephut - Courtesy of
https://commons.wikimedia.org/wiki/File:Hatshepsut_Temple_R05.jpg -
This file is licensed under the Creative Commons Attribution-Share Alike
4.0 international license.

118.	Temple Of Hatshephut - Courtesy of
https://en.wikipedia.org/wiki/File:Hatshetsup-temple-1by7.jpg - This file
is licensed under the Creative Commons Attribution-Share Alike 3.0
Unported license.

119.	Pharaoh Thuthmose III – Courtesy of
https://commons.wikimedia.org/wiki/File:Thutmose_III_sphinx-E_10897-
IMG_0040-gradient.jpg - This file is licensed under the Creative
Commons Attribution-Share Alike 2.0 France license..

120.	Egyptian Empire under reign of Pharaoh Thuthmose III –
Courtesy of https://www.britannica.com/biography/Thutmose-III – This
image is in the Public Domain.

121.	Pharaoh Thuthmose III – Courtesy of
https://commons.wikimedia.org/wiki/File:Thutmosis_III_wien_front.jpg –
This image is in the Public Domain

122.	Pharaoh Thuthmose III – Courtesy of
https://commons.wikimedia.org/wiki/File:Thutmose_III,_Luxor_Museum.
jpg - This file is licensed under the Creative Commons Attribution-Share
Alike 4.0 international license.

123.	Pharaoh Amenhotep II – Courtesy of
https://commons.wikimedia.org/wiki/File:Amenhotep_II,_18th_dynasty,_
Ny_Carlsberg_Glyptotek,_Copenhagen_(4)_(36252715572).jpg - This
file is licensed under the Creative Commons Attribution-Share Alike 2.0
Generic license.

124.	Pharaoh Amenhotep II – Courtesy of
https://commons.wikimedia.org/wiki/File:Idealised_portrait_head_of_pha
raoh_Amenophis_II_with_nemes_02.jpg - This file is licensed under the
Creative Commons Attribution-Share Alike 4.0 International license.

125.	Pharaoh Amenhotep II – Courtesy of
https://commons.wikimedia.org/wiki/File:Amenhotep_II,_ca._1439-
1413_BCE,_Amenhotep_II,_18th_dynasty,_Ny_Carlsberg_Glyptotek,_C
openhagen_(2)_(36376057866).jpg - This file is licensed under the
Creative Commons Attribution-Share Alike 2.0 Generic license.

126.	Pharaoh Amenhotep II – Courtesy of
https://commons.wikimedia.org/wiki/File:Idealised_portrait_head_of_pha
raoh_Amenophis_II_with_nemes_02.jpg - This file is licensed under the
Creative Commons Attribution-Share Alike 4.0 International license.

127.   Pharaoh Amenhotep II – Courtesy of https://commons.wikimedia.org/wiki/File:Bust_of_Amenhotep_II_%C3%84gyptisches_Museum_Berlin.jpg - This file is licensed under the Creative Commons Attribution-Share Alike 3.0 Unported license.

128.   Pharaoh Amenhotep II – Courtesy of https://www.metmuseum.org/art/collection/search/545891 – This image is in the Public Domain

129.   Pharaoh Thuthmose IV – Courtesy of https://commons.wikimedia.org/wiki/File:Thutmosis_IV_wearing_the_blue_war_crown_of_Egypt.jpg - This file is licensed under the Creative Commons Attribution-Share Alike 4.0 International license.

130.   Pharaoh Thuthmose IV – Courtesy of https://commons.wikimedia.org/wiki/File:Thumtmoses_IV-E_13889-IMG_0034-gradient.jpg - This file is licensed under the Creative Commons Attribution-Share Alike 3.0 France license.

131.   Pharaoh Thuthmose IV & Anubis – Courtesy of - https://sk.m.wikipedia.org/wiki/S%C3%BAbor:VdR_TIV9.jpg - This file is licensed under the Creative Commons Attribution-Share Alike 3.0 Unported license.

132.   Pharaoh Amenhotep III – Courtesy of https://www.metmuseum.org/art/collection/search/544477 – This image is in the Public Domain

133.   Pharaoh Amenhotep III – Courtesy of https://commons.wikimedia.org/wiki/File:Pharaon_amenophis_3_egypt_a-2.jpg - This file is licensed under the Creative Commons Attribution-Share Alike 3.0 Unported license.

134.   Pharaoh Amenhotep III – Courtesy of https://www.metmuseum.org/art/collection/search/544477 - This image is in the Public Domain

135.   Pharaoh Amenhotep III – Courtesy of https://www.flickr.com/photos/prof_richard/40402235193 - Attribution 2.0 Generic (CC BY 2.0)

136.   Pharaoh Amenhotep III – Courtesy of https://flickr.com/photos/43714545@N06/40223629841- Attribution 2.0 Generic (CC BY 2.0)

137.   Pharaoh Amenhotep III – Courtesy of https://es.m.wikipedia.org/wiki/Archivo:British_Museum_Egypt_074.jpg - This file is licensed under the Creative Commons Attribution-Share Alike 3.0 Unported, 2.5 Generic, 2.0 Generic and 1.0 Generic license.

138.   Queen Tiye – Courtesy of https://commons.wikimedia.org/wiki/File:Queen_Tiy_N2312_E25493_mp3h8763.jpg - This file is licensed under the Creative Commons Attribution-Share Alike 2.0 France license..

139.   Queen Tiye – Courtesy of https://commons.wikimedia.org/wiki/File:Portrait_de_la_reine_Tiyi_Neues_Museum_Berlin_26042018_1.jpg – This image is in the Public Domain

166

140.   Queen Tiye – Courtesy of -
https://en.wikipedia.org/wiki/Tiye#/media/File:Relief_of_Queen_Tiye,_w
earing_the_vulture_headdress_and_uraeus._From_the_mortuary_temple_
of_Amenhotep_III_at_Western_Thebes,_Egypt,_c._1375_BCE._Neues_
Museum.jpg - This file is licensed under the Creative Commons
Attribution-Share Alike 4.0 International license.

141.   Queen Tiye – Courtesy of
https://commons.wikimedia.org/wiki/File:Queen_Tiye,_Great_Royal_Wif
e_bust,_18th_dynasty.jpg - This file is licensed under the Creative
Commons Attribution-Share Alike 4.0 International license.

142.   Queen Tiye – Courtesy of
https://commons.wikimedia.org/wiki/File:Head_of_Queen_Tiye,_wearing
_the_double-feathered_crown_with_the_sun-disc_and_Hathor
%27s_horns._From_Medinet_el-
Ghurob,_Egypt._C._1355_BCE._Neues_Museum.jpg - This file is
licensed under the Creative Commons Attribution-Share Alike 4.0
International license.

143.   Queen Tiye – Courtesy of
https://commons.wikimedia.org/wiki/File:Queen_Tiye_-_cropped_-
_probably_with_her_husband_Amenhotep_III_-_34_louvre_-
_egyptarchive.JPG – This image is in the Public Domain.

144.   Pharaoh Akhenaten – Courtesy of
https://commons.wikimedia.org/wiki/File:ReliefPortraitOfAkhenaten01.p
ng - This file is licensed under the Creative Commons Attribution-Share
Alike 3.0 Unported license.

145.   Pharaoh Akhenaten – Courtesy of
https://www.flickr.com/photos/leswilliamsphotography/15462699390 -
Attribution-ShareAlike 2.0 Generic (CC BY-SA 2.0)

146.   Pharaoh Akhenaten – Courtesy of
https://commons.wikimedia.org/wiki/File:Luxor_Museum_Statuenkopf_E
chnaton_02.jpg - This file is licensed under the Creative Commons
Attribution-Share Alike 3.0 Unported license.

147.   Pharaoh Akhenaten – Courtesy of
https://www.metmuseum.org/art/collection/search/544528 – This image is
in the Public Domain

148.   Pharaoh Akhenaten – Courtesy of
https://commons.wikimedia.org/wiki/File:Nuovo_regno,_xviii_dinastia,_r
egno_di_amenhotep_IV,_ritratto_di_nefertiti_talatat,_da_karnak_1353-
1347_ac_ca.jpg - This file is licensed under the Creative Commons
Attribution-Share Alike 3.0 Unported license.

149.   Pharaoh Akhenaten – Courtesy of
https://commons.wikimedia.org/wiki/File:Akhenaten_modell_head_replic
a_smaller.jpg - This file is licensed under the Creative Commons
Attribution-Share Alike 4.0 international, 2.5 Generic, 2.0 Generic and 1.0
Generic license.

150.   Queen Nefertiti – Courtesy of
https://fr.m.wikipedia.org/wiki/Fichier:Nuovo_regno,_xviii_dinastia,_reg

no_di_amenhotep_IV,_ritratto_di_nefertiti,_da_karnak_1353-1347_ac_ca.jpg – This file is licensed under the Creative Commons Attribution-Share Alike 3.0 Unported license.

151.   Queen Nefertiti – Courtesy of https://commons.wikimedia.org/wiki/File:Queen_Nefertiti,_Limestone_relief.jpg – This image is in the Public Domain

152.   Queen Nefertiti – Courtesy of https://commons.wikimedia.org/wiki/File:Unfinished_model_head_of_a_statue_of_Nefertiti,_18th_dynasty,_1351-1334_BC,_Neues_Museum,_Berlin_(8169140401).jpg - This file is licensed under the Creative Commons Attribution-Share Alike 2.0 Generic license.

153.   Queen Nefertiti – Courtesy of https://www.metmuseum.org/art/collection/search/545803 – This image is in the Public Domain

154.   Queen Nefertiti – Courtesy of https://commons.wikimedia.org/wiki/File:WLA_brooklynmuseum_Nefertiti_ca_1352-1336_BCE.jpg - This file is licensed under the Creative Commons Attribution-Share Alike 2.5 Generic license.

155.   Queen Nefertiti – Courtesy of https://commons.wikimedia.org/wiki/File:Portrait_head_of_queen_Nefertiti.jpg -This file is licensed under the Creative Commons Attribution-Share Alike 4.0 international license.

156.   Pharaoh Akhenaten worshipping the "Aten" - Courtesy of https://commons.wikimedia.org/wiki/File:La_salle_dAkhenaton_(1356-1340_av_J.C.)_(Mus%C3%A9e_du_Caire)_(2076972086).jpg – This image is in the Public Domain

157.   Akhenaten, Nefertiti & their children – Courtesy of https://commons.wikimedia.org/wiki/File:Akhenaten,_Nefertiti_and_their_children.jpg – This image is in the Public Domain.

158.   Queen Meritaten – Courtesy of https://commons.wikimedia.org/wiki/File:Princess_of_Akhenaton_family-E_14715-IMG_0319-gradient.jpg - This file is licensed under the Creative Commons Attribution-Share Alike 3.0 France license.

159.   Queen Meritaten – Courtesy of https://www.brooklynmuseum.org/opencollection/objects/3699 - This file is licensed under the Creative Commons Attribution-Share Alike 2.5 Generic license.

160.   Pharaoh Tutankhamun – Courtesy of https://commons.wikimedia.org/wiki/File:Tutanhkamun_tomb_statue_edit_1.jpg – This image is in the Public Domain

161.   Pharaoh Tutankhamun – Courtesy of https://commons.wikimedia.org/wiki/File:Head_of_King_Tutankhamen-11.1533-IMG_4848-gradient.jpg - This file is licensed under the Creative Commons Attribution-Share Alike 2.0 France license.

162.   Pharaoh Tutankhamun – Courtesy of https://commons.wikimedia.org/wiki/File:Buste_de_Tout

%C3%A2nkhamon_(mus
%C3%A9e_du_Caire_Egypte)_(1815597310).jpg - This file is licensed under the Creative Commons Attribution-Share Alike 2.0 Generic license.

163.   Pharaoh Tutankhamun – Courtesy of https://commons.wikimedia.org/wiki/File:Tutanhkamun_Shabti.jpg – This image is in the Public Domain

164.   Pharaoh Tutankhamun – Courtesy of https://commons.wikimedia.org/wiki/File:Toutankamon-expo_48_masque.JPG - This file is licensed under the Creative Commons Attribution-Share Alike 3.0 Unported license.

165.   Pharaoh Tutankhamun – Courtesy of https://commons.wikimedia.org/wiki/File:T%C3%AAte_de_Tout %C3%A2nkhamon_enfant_(mus%C3%A9e_du_Caire_Egypte).jpg - This file is licensed under the Creative Commons Attribution-Share Alike 2.0 Generic license.

166.   Pharaoh Tutankhamun Embraces Osiris – Courtesy of https://commons.wikimedia.org/wiki/File:Tutankhamun_embraces_Osiris. jpg – This image is in the Public Domain

167.   Pharaoh Tutankhamun & his wife Ankhesenamun – Courtesy of https://commons.wikimedia.org/wiki/File:Tutankhamun_and_his_wife.jpg - This file is licensed under the Creative Commons Attribution-Share Alike 4.0 International license.

168.   Pharaoh Ay – Courtesy of https://www.flickr.com/photos/ddenisen/7179205803/in/photostream/ - Attribution-ShareAlike 2.0 Generic (CC BY-SA 2.0)

169.   Pharaoh Ay – Courtesy of https://commons.wikimedia.org/wiki/File:Opening_of_the_Mouth_-_Tutankhamun_and_Aja-2.jpg – This image is in the Public Domain

170.   Pharaoh Horemheb – Courtesy of https://www.flickr.com/photos/72746018@N00/2080460674 - Attribution 2.0 Generic (CC BY 2.0)

171.   Pharaoh Horemheb – Courtesy of https://www.wikiwand.com/et/Horemheb - Attribution-ShareAlike 2.0 Generic (CC BY-SA 2.0

172.   Pharaoh Ramses I – Courtesy of https://commons.wikimedia.org/wiki/File:Statue_Paramesses_Munich.JP G - This file is licensed under the Creative Commons Attribution-Share Alike 4.0 International license.

173.   Pharaoh Ramses I – Courtesy of https://en.wikipedia.org/wiki/Ramesses_I - This file is licensed under the Creative Commons Attribution-Share Alike 2.5 Generic license.

174.   Pharaoh Seti I – Courtesy of https://commons.wikimedia.org/wiki/File:Seti_I_Temple_Reliefs_at_Aby dos_(VIII).jpg - This file is licensed under the Creative Commons Attribution-Share Alike 2.0 Generic license.

175.   Pharaoh Seti I – Courtesy of

https://commons.wikimedia.org/wiki/File:Nuovo_regno,_la_dea_hathor_a ccoglie_seth_I,_dalla_valle_dei_re,_1294-1279_ac_ca.JPG - This file is licensed under the Creative Commons Attribution-Share Alike 3.0 Unported license

176.   Pharaoh Seti I before Thoth – Courtesy of https://commons.wikimedia.org/wiki/File:KV17,_the_tomb_of_Pharaoh_ Seti_I_of_the_Nineteenth_Dynasty,_Burial_chamber_J,_the_King_before _Thot,_Valley_of_the_Kings,_Egypt_(49845802023).jpg - This file is licensed under the Creative Commons Attribution-Share Alike 2.0 Generic license.

177.   Pharaoh Ramses II – Courtesy of https://commons.wikimedia.org/wiki/File:Bust_of_King_Ramses_II_00_(7).jpg - This file is licensed under the Creative Commons Attribution-Share Alike 4.0 International license.

178.   Pharaoh Ramses II – Courtesy of https://commons.wikimedia.org/wiki/File:Abu_Simbel_008.jpg - This file is licensed under the Creative Commons Attribution-Share Alike 3.0 Unported license.

179.   Pharaoh Ramses II – Courtesy of https://commons.wikimedia.org/wiki/File:Manchester_Museum_2015_02 5_-_King_Ramesses_II.jpg - This file is licensed under the Creative Commons Attribution-Share Alike 4.0 international license – Photograph by Mike Peel – www.mikepeel.net

180.   Pharaoh Ramses II – Courtesy of https://commons.wikimedia.org/wiki/File:Statue_de_Ramses_II.jpg - This file is licensed under the Creative Commons Attribution-Share Alike 4.0 international license.

181.   Queen Ahmose Nefertari – Courtesy of https://commons.wikimedia.org/wiki/File:Queen_Ahmes_Nefertari- E_11232-IMG_2876.JPG - This file is licensed under the Creative Commons Attribution-Share Alike 3.0 France license.

182.   Queen Ahmose Nefertari – Courtesy of https://commons.wikimedia.org/wiki/File:Queen_Ahmose- Nefertari_Neues_Museum_26042018_1.jpg - This file is made available under the creative commons CC0 1.0 Universal Public Domain.

183.   Queen Ahmose Nefertari – Courtesy of https://commons.wikimedia.org/wiki/File:Qeen_Nefertari.JPG – This file is licensed under the Creative Commons Attribution-Share Alike 4.0 international license Attribution: Kingtut at Hungarian Wikipedia

184.   Queen Ahmose Nefertari – Courtesy of https://flickr.com/photos/86012097@N08/24008364551 – This image is in the Public Domain

185.   Queen Ahmose Nefertari Paying Senet – Courtesy of https://www.metmuseum.org/art/collection/search/548355 - This image is in the Public Domain

186.   Pharaoh Ramses II's Temple At Abu Simbel – Courtesy of https://commons.wikimedia.org/wiki/File:Abu_Simbel_Temple_May_30_

2007.jpg – This image is in the Public Domain

187.　　　Pharaoh Ramses II's Temple At Abu Simbel – Courtesy of
https://commons.wikimedia.org/wiki/File:Abu_Simbel,_Ramesses_Templ
e,_front,_Egypt,_Oct_2004.jpg - This file is licensed under the Creative
Commons Attribution-Share Alike 2.0 Generic license.

188.　　　Temple Of Hathor & Nefertari – Courtesy of -
https://flickr.com/photos/22490717@N02/2217474194 - This file is
licensed under the Creative Commons Attribution-Share Alike 2.0
Generic license

189.　　　Temple Of Hathor & Nefertari – Courtesy of
https://flickr.com/photos/59081381@N03/48016877176 – This image is
in the Public Domain

190.　　　Pharaoh Merneptah – Courtesy of
https://commons.wikimedia.org/wiki/File:Merneptah_-
_Thorvaldsens_Museum_-_DSC08745.JPG – This image is in the Public
Domain

191.　　　Pharaoh Merneptah – Courtesy of
https://www.metmuseum.org/art/collection/search/548352 - This image is
in the Public Domain

192.　　　Pharaoh Seti II – Courtesy of
https://commons.wikimedia.org/wiki/File:Turin_statue_of_Seti_II.jpg -
This file is licensed under the Creative Commons Attribution-Share Alike
2.0 Generic license.

193.　　　Pharaoh Seti II – Courtesy of
https://www.metmuseum.org/art/collection/search/544752 – This image is
in the Public Domain

194.　　　Pharaoh Amenmesse – Courtesy of
https://commons.wikimedia.org/wiki/File:St%C3%A8le,_NE_01a.jpg -
This file is licensed under the Creative Commons Attribution-Share Alike
3.0 Unported license.

195.　　　Pharaoh Siptah – Courtesy of
https://commons.wikimedia.org/wiki/File:Wall_paintings_in_Siptah
%27s_tomb,_Valley_of_Kings.jpg - This file is licensed under the
Creative Commons Attribution-Share Alike 3.0 Unported license. Subject
to disclaimers

196.　　　Pharaoh Siptah – Courtesy of
https://commons.wikimedia.org/wiki/File:Siptah.jpg - This file is licensed
under the Creative Commons Attribution-Share Alike 3.0 Unported
license.

197.　　　Pharaoh Twosret – Courtesy of
https://commons.wikimedia.org/wiki/File:Twosret.jpg - This file is
licensed under the Creative Commons Attribution-Share Alike 3.0
Unported license.

198.　　　Pharaoh Setnakhte – Courtesy of
https://commons.wikimedia.org/wiki/File:Funerary_Papyrus_of_the_Stew
ard_Sethnakht_MET_35.9.19a-e_EGDP010489.jpg – This image is in the
Public Domain

199.   Pharaoh Setnakhte – Courtesy of https://commons.wikimedia.org/wiki/File:Sethnakht_closeup_Lepsius.png - This image is in the Public Domain

200.   Pharaoh Ramses III – Courtesy of https://commons.wikimedia.org/wiki/File:KhonsuTemple-Karnak-RamessesIII-2.jpg - This file is licensed under the Creative Commons Attribution-Share Alike 3.0 Unported license.

201.   Pharaoh Ramses III – Courtesy of https://commons.wikimedia.org/wiki/File:KhonsuTemple-Karnak-RamessesIII-2.jpg - This file is licensed under the Creative Commons Attribution-Share Alike 3.0 Unported license.

202.   Pharaoh Ramses IV - Courtesy of https://commons.wikimedia.org/wiki/File:Detail._Upper_part_of_a_kneeling_figure_of_Ramesses_IV_holding_a_nw-bowl_in_each_hand._Greywacke._New_Kingdom,_20th_Dynasty,_1153-1147_BCE._Probably_from_Thebes,_possibly_from_the_Temple_of_Amun_at_Karnak._British_Museum.jpg - This file is licensed under the Creative Commons Attribution-Share Alike 4.0 International license.

203.   Map Of Egypt 25th Dynasty – Courtesy of https://commons.wikimedia.org/wiki/File:Kushite_heartland_and_Kushite_Empire_of_the_25th_dynasty_circa_700_BCE.jpg - This file is licensed under the Creative Commons Attribution-Share Alike 4.0 International license.

204.   Pharaoh Shabaqa – Courtesy of https://en.wikipedia.org/wiki/Shabaka - https://www.flickr.com/photos/scgkid/8099058414/in/photostream/ - Attribution-ShareAlike 2.0 Generic (CC BY-SA 2.0)

205.   Pharaoh Shabaqa – Courtesy of https://commons.wikimedia.org/wiki/File:CabezaDeShabaka_(46149518542).jpg - This file is licensed under the Creative Commons Attribution-Share Alike 2.0 Generic license

206.   Pharaoh Shebitku – Courtesy of https://commons.wikimedia.org/wiki/File:Shebitku%E2%80%99s_statue_(Nubian_Museum).jpg - This file is licensed under the Creative Commons Attribution 2.0 Generic license

207.   Pharaoh Taharqa – Courtesy of https://commons.wikimedia.org/wiki/File:Bm_taharqa.jpg - This file is licensed under the Creative Commons Attribution-Share Alike 3.0 Unported license

208.   Pharaoh Taharqa – Courtesy of https://www.flickr.com/photos/prof_richard/36420740125/ - Attribution 2.0 Generic (CC BY 2.0)

209.   Pharaoh Taharqa – Courtesy of – This image is in the Public Domain.

210.   Pharaoh Taharqa – Courtesy of https://commons.wikimedia.org/wiki/File:Shabti_of_King_Taharqa.jpg - This file is licensed under the Creative Commons Attribution-Share Alike

3.0 Unported, 2.5 Generic, 2.0 Generic and 1.0 Generic license.

211.   Pharaoh Tantamani – Courtesy of https://commons.wikimedia.org/wiki/File:Tantamani_closeup.jpg - This file is licensed under the Creative Commons Attribution-Share Alike 4.0 International license

212.   Pharaoh Tantamani – Courtesy of https://commons.wikimedia.org/wiki/File:Tantamani_profile.jpg - This file is licensed under the Creative Commons Attribution-Share Alike 3.0 Unported license.

213.   Pharaoh Tantamani – Courtesy of https://commons.wikimedia.org/wiki/File:Portrait_of_Tantamani_in_his_t omb_in_El-Kurru.jpg – This image is in the Public Domain.

214.   Pharaoh Tantamani – Courtesy of https://www.flickr.com/photos/tobeyfootsteps/49164690351/ - Attribution-ShareAlike 2.0 Generic (CC BY-SA 2.0)

215.   God Amun – Courtesy of https://commons.wikimedia.org/wiki/File:Luxor_Museum_Relief_Amun-Min_01.jpg - This file is licensed under the Creative Commons Attribution-Share Alike 3.0 Unported license.

216.   God Amun – Courtesy https://commons.wikimedia.org/wiki/File:StatueHeadOfGodAmun-LikenessOfTutankhamun_MetropolitanMuseum.png - This file is licensed under the Creative Commons Attribution-Share Alike 4.0 International license.

217.   God Ptah – Courtesy of https://commons.wikimedia.org/wiki/File:Ptah-A_2004-33-IMG_0951.JPG - This file is licensed under the Creative Commons Attribution-Share Alike 2.0 France license.

218.   God Ptah – Courtesy of https://commons.wikimedia.org/wiki/File:Head,_Ptah_MET_m2600_fron t.jpg – This image is in the Public Domain.

219.   Goddess Hathor – Courtresy of https://www.metmuseum.org/art/collection/search/551039 -This image is in the Public Domain.

220.   Goddess Hathor – Courtresy of https://commons.wikimedia.org/wiki/File:MC_-_Hathor.jpg - This file is licensed under the Creative - Share Alike 3.0 Unported, 2.5 Generic, 2.0 Generic and 1.0 Generic license.

221.   Goddes Isis – Courtesy of https://commons.wikimedia.org/wiki/File:Statuette_of_Isis_nursing_Horu s_(missing_above_the_legs),_inscribed_for_Hor_son_of_Padihorresnet_ MET_DP139139.jpg – This image is in the Public Domain.

222.   Goddes Isis – Courtesy of https://commons.wikimedia.org/wiki/File:Statuette_of_Isis_and_Horus_ MET_04.2.585.jpg -This image is in the Public Domain

223.　　　　God Hapy – Courtesy of https://commons.wikimedia.org/wiki/File:Statue_of_the_Nile-god_Hapy,_British_Museum.jpg - https://www.flickr.com/photos/64671288@N00/4500903994 - This file is licensed under the Creative Commons Attribution 2.0 Generic license

224.　　　　God Hapy – Courtesy of https://commons.wikimedia.org/wiki/File:Limestone_slab_showing_the_Nile_flood_god_Hapy._12th_Dynasty._From_the_foundations_of_the_te mple_of_Thutmose_III,_Koptos,_Egypt._The_Petrie_Museum_of_Egypti an_Archaeology,_London.jpg - This file is licensed under the Creative Commons Attribution-Share Alike 4.0 International license.

225.　　　　God Khonsu – Courtesy of https://commons.wikimedia.org/wiki/File:Statue_Khonsu_Weigall.jpg – This image is in the Public Domain.

226.　　　　God Khonsu – Courtesy of https://commons.wikimedia.org/wiki/File:Cairo_Museum_%E9%96%8B %E7%BE%85%E5%8D%9A%E7%89%A9%E9%A4%A8_-_panoramio.jpg – attribution lienyuan lee https://web.archive.org/web/20161027162316/http://www.panoramio.com /photo/107193619 - This file is licensed under the Creative Commons Attribution 3.0 Unported license.

227.　　　　God Osiris – Courtesy of https://commons.wikimedia.org/wiki/File:Osiris_E3751_mp3h8829-b.jpg - This file is licensed under the Creative Commons Attribution-ShareAlike 3.0 France license

228.　　　　God Osiris – Courtesy of https://commons.wikimedia.org/wiki/File:Statue_du_dieu_Osiris.jpg – This image is in the Public Domain.

ABOUT THE AUTHOR

Truth B. Tole had no intentions of writing a book about the ancient Egyptians. However, when the serious backlash, received at the mere mention of the ancient Egyptians being black people from Africa was displayed over and over again, the seeds of this book were planted.

It is not the opinion of Truth B. Tole that the ancient Egyptians were black people, these are easily proveable facts.

Even more revealing is that, in conversations about the race of the ancient Egyptians with many who claim a non black anicent Egypt, it becomes clear that these people have never done any actual research on the topic. They have never done a deep dive or searched for a clue as to what the ancient Egyptians, the pyramid builders, actually looked like. They have instead taken the words of those in positions of authority, hollywood movies and the media as the main source of their information.

As a result, Truth B. Tole and this book was born. The motivation for this book is to raise the level of consciousness of all people as to the rich and ancient history of black people.

They say a picture is worth a thousand words. We hope you agree.

www.ingramcontent.com/pod-product-compliance
Lightning Source LLC
Chambersburg PA
CBHW070919270326
41927CB00011B/2639